After the City

Lars Lerup

The MIT Press

Cambridge, Massachusetts

London, England

This book was set in Helvetica and was printed and bound in the United States of America.

Library of Congress Cataloging-in-Publication Data

Lerup, Lars.
  . After the city / Lars Lerup.
        p. cm.
    Includes bibliographical references and index.
    ISBN 0-262-12224-3 (hc : alk. paper)
      1. City planning—History—20th century. 2. City planning—Philosophy. 3. Metropolitan areas. 4. Suburbs. 5. Architecture, Modern—20th century. I. Title.

NA9095.L47 2000
720—dc21   99-056867

For the sailors of my youth, who told me about the vast oceans,
Frisco, Pancho, and Shanghai

Contents

Acknowledgments

I especially want to thank:

Sanford Kwinter and Stephen Fox for their brilliant admixture of criticism, enthusiasm, and editorial suggestions.

Michael Bell, Aaron Betsky, John Biln, Farés el Dahdah, Edward Dimendberg, Albert Pope, and Frederick Turner for their support, patient listening, and important comments.

Dung Ngo for earlier developments of text and image.

Kim Shoemake and Luke Bulman for their invaluable assistance with the look of the book.

Doris Anderson and Janet Wheeler for their support.

Roger Conover of the MIT Press, whose astonishing twenty-year list I am very proud to be part of, and my editor Matthew Abbate and designer Jim McWethy.

I also want to thank President Malcolm Gillis and former Provost David Auston of Rice University for their active support of a *working* dean. I can think of no better setting for creative work than this great university. I especially want to thank John Casbarian. His friendship and support of my creative work combined with his exquisite associate deanship makes my life at Rice a pleasure. I want to acknowledge all of the wild developers and builders who created Houston, without whom this book would not have been possible. Finally, I want to thank my family who have suffered stoically the ups and downs of the author.

Houston, November 1999

The Metropolis: A Portfolio of Images

1 *Rear view*

A sudden glimpse, a distant bearing, a momentary stop on the eye's endless loop: roadway, neighboring traffic, instruments, your passenger. The optic pouch explodes instantly into the distance to envelop the megashape of downtown, retrieving it for short-term storage, mapping it onto the construction site of memory, only to cut the shape loose until the next encounter.

2 *Gulfgate Shopping City*

"Born to shop," the stimmers spill off the freeway to evaporate in the parking lot. The assemblage of car/credit card/shopper is the hypodermic of the shopping stream. Just as the medieval stirrup transferred the power of the horse to the horseman's lance, the shopping assemblage composes and releases pure buying power. Whatever the hour, day or night, the stimmers' time is always now. As a place, the mall is a feverish monad held up only by its intoxicating inside.

3 *Sick City, the Texas Medical Center*

A fleet of air and ground vehicles, elevators, and stretchers delivers the medical body. The ecology of prevention, care, and intervention operates on world time—twenty-four hours a day, seven days a week. Bodies come and go, live and die. Free parking at first visit. Brain scan, bone scan, MRI, PSA, hopes, illusions, and the eternal wait. Statistics vs. self.

4 Depth and height

The oil gusher is transfigured and petrified in the priapic
tower—the emptying of the earth and the filling of the sky.

5 *Preparation and promise*

The prefiguration of the metropolis as a holey space soon to be filled. The clean slate includes the city floor, the weather system, and the facsimiles of what's to come (or what could be): the Warwick Hotel at the edge of Hermann Park.

6 *Minor air show*

Lifting out of the ground, the freeway abandons its base
to join, ever so briefly, the air space. Helicopters join Suburbans in the minor air show.

7 *Skeletons*

The corner columns, essential to the skeletal structure inside the distant Transco Tower (designed by Johnson and
Burgee), were removed from the early plans, at the
client's request, to make the ubiquitous corner office
more attractive. This required deeper and wider can-
tilevered perimeter beams that in turn limited the placement of lighting to the ceiling bay behind. Lighting is made
possible by electricity delivered via the skeletal towers in
the foreground, which also deliver electricity to the stoves
in the homes in the middle ground, allowing the preparation of meat from cows almost identical to the cow in the
foreground. Its erect position is made possible by another
skeleton, visible only once the cow is stripped of its flesh.

8 *Air space*

Between desire and action: The huge and volatile air bag rests like a pillow over the metropolis. Deceptively inviting in good weather; even the weariest get no rest when Canadian air confronts its Mexican double. In Houston air has a special taste, a special promise, a special desire: a mixture of roughneck and astronaut dreams, of helicopters (heading for the rigs at sea) and space vehicles. Wealth and adventure. Texas action.

9 *Demolition derby*

The subconscious of the freeway mind fulfills its wildest
dream. At the center are oil, grease, smoke, roaring engines, and the crashing of metal, while the crowd hovers
on the perimeter in the darkness beneath the giant skull-
cap of the Astrodome. Gladiators, bullfighters, rodeo riders, all are destined to meet in mortal embrace, making
the arena a historical place: the end of the line. The ultimate behavioral sink: here we are born again to destroy
at the end of the cul-de-sac of time and motion.

10 *Sound and fury*

If we could only hear the thunder—the hissing, the crackling, and the echoes—the flatness of the image would disappear in favor of a space whose confinements are mysteriously created by content rather than extent—the ur-architecture of the metropolis.

11 *The zoohemic canopy*

Planning Principle I: When in doubt, plant a tree.

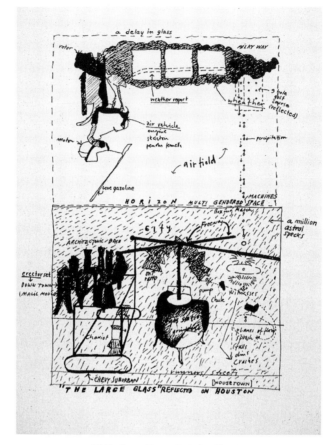

12 *The* Large Glass *reflected on Houston*

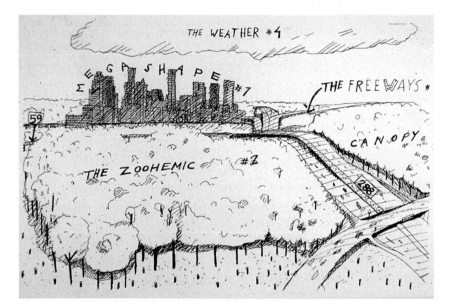

13 *Megashapes*

14 *Miasma*

When Friedrich Engels inspected the innermost courts of
Manchester in search of working-class life, he was as-
tounded to find that he could not feel the ground under his
feet because of the refuse and debris. The modern wanderer may feel similarly on days when the yellowish miasma
hides the horizon, burns the eyes, and stings the throat.

15 *Extensions*

The vast flatness of the Texas landscape welds ground space and air space seamlessly. The new space confuses fish and fowl, particularly when the zoohemic canopy is broken. In this vehicular paradise, cars are loved, helicopters smiled at, airplanes adored, and airships revered. In Finland, where everyone seems to have one, the mobile phone's street name has changed from "yuppie teddy bear" to "hand extension." In Houston, the Suburban (with its hood open in the foreground) is the exoskeleton of the suburbanites and the movable extension of their habitat.

16 *Superhighway*

Thirty-four man-years are spent per day commuting on the freeways in Houston. Yet the ride heals, soothes, and eases the jump cuts between home and work, between nature and culture, between byway and freeway, between his and hers.

I
Introduction

Tafuri's Smile

In large part this book originates in experience, and my overall intention is pragmatic, despite its often philosophical orientation. Having left Berkeley, California, and its peculiar insularity for Houston, Texas, in 1993, I realized that for the first time I had encountered what Manfredo Tafuri, the Italian architectural theorist and historian, called "the merciless commercialization of the human environment": America and the suburban metropolis.[1]

This encounter was fraught with conflict, fascination, and repulsion. Yet in retrospect it was cathartic and deeply liberating. Upon confronting the metropolis, my "ambiguous conscience"—my resistance—was slowly, then radically transformed into pragmatism and new hope, particularly for the generations of students—future architects—who have been in my life for so many years. The book attempts to cover the ground between city and design, succinctly rather than exhaustively because the subject is so vast and because of my lack of patience and my desire to make a comprehensible project that is open and accessible, filled with lacunas and incipient trajectories.

I must confess to having read a few books many times and not the other way around. Tafuri's *Architecture and Utopia* is one of those books. On each reading it is almost a new book. Tafuri haunted me. His devastating reading of the modern city and its architecture convinced me for years that architecture was dead. Yet it was the perplexing ambiguity of the text that was the source of my unease. As though it were an inkblot test, *Architecture and Utopia* became a reflection of my struggles with the discipline and the profession. Each new significant encounter in my world of architecture suggested a slightly different reading of Tafuri. His text rarely coincided fully with my experiences, or with the demands on me as a teacher of architecture. However, since the general malaise of the architect on the heels of the turmoil of the 1960s did coincide with Tafuri's reading of the discipline, the impact of his book was that of a conscience that kept me up at night—the four o'clock wolf hour—while it stayed away during the day. Despite my nightly doubts, I was able to design an array of architectural projects. But they were haunted by my fear of producing what he called "exasperated objects"—objects of pure form that in their baroque formfulness disguised the fact that they had nothing to say. My projects were always full of intended meaning. In retrospect the projects were "heroic" attempts to break the media constraints of architectural form, to make form write. Invariably the projects became wedded to the dwellers because only the latter could bring meaning to life "in speech and action" (Arendt). This proved consequential, since the complex of subject-object relations was to become my path to liberation. Tafuri's conclusions in *Architecture and Utopia* were full of despair. After a personal crisis he abandoned the modern project for the nobler and safer pursuit of history. The last time I saw him, he looked at me enigmatically with a hint of a smile. Since I didn't know him well I did not know what he was hinting at.

In Houston, residing on the 28th floor of a high-rise building—*bien au-dessus de la mêlée*—I see graphically how architecture had been "pitilessly absorbed" by the metropolis. Tafuri's book came again into focus, rallying around his main topics: the Shock of the Metropolis, Reason's Adventures, and Problems in the Form of a Conclusion. The city's "will to formlessness," in short, the reckless forces of market-driven development oblivious to the plan, have almost obliterated architecture here as it had been understood historically: "a stable structure, which gives form to permanent values and consolidates urban morphology."[2] Our "permanent values" have lost their permanence and their manifestation in the city fabric. Tafuri's apocalyptic conclusion of this liquidation of the importance of architecture seemed, in the throes of the forever-changing metropolis, less consequential. Gianni Vattimo, the Italian philosopher of hermeneutics, describes our farewell to modernity as a convalescence from sickness: we have become used to architecture that is no longer the instrument of city form.[3] Consequently the "necessary reconciliation between the mobility of values and the stability of [architecture's] principles" has become less necessary. In a world ruled by suburban values and market pragmatism, it is possible that mobile values have found a new if momentary home in the single-family house on its lot along a meandering street in the suburban enclave. And in this particular algorithm architecture clearly plays second fiddle. The static resistance of traditional architecture in the face of radical mobility demands rethinking rather than escape. After all, the historian's library is not an option for practicing architects.

My essay "Stim & Dross: Rethinking the Metropolis," written while still shocked by Houston, is our theater of operation. Rewritten, expanded, and tampered with, it is the book's plot, a plot that invites questions about theory and action. In the essay I make a clear distinction between city and metropolis. As this book's title *After the City* suggests, the metropolis has replaced the city, and as a consequence architecture as a static enterprise has been displaced by architecture as a form of software (a suggestion posed at the outset as a mild provocation). The trajectory of the old city was toward complete and utter artifice (think of nature in Paris or Rome!); the (suburban) metropolis points in the opposite direction, toward nature, or should we say toward the preternatural alloy of nature and artifice. The metropolis's inclination toward nature has distinct historical connections with Enlightenment architectural theory, specifically that of Abbé Laugier and his suggestion that the city should be reduced to natural phenomena. The inclination was one of formal resemblance, best demonstrated by the English picturesque. In the modern metropolis nature takes a more pragmatic and complex position, particularly when it appears that ecology may be the only viable challenge to market economics. This is particularly relevant in the metropolis, since from its modern beginning nature was part of the original equation, due to the low density—the relation between built and open space—of the single-family house. In such conurbations as Los Angeles and Houston, this equation is still dominated by nature. But only in terms of acreage (forgetting for a moment earthquakes, hurricanes, and floods), since artifice in its intensity and insidious dominance has long since blotted out the night sky and almost silenced the birds. The challenge is to rethink and reactivate the equation, which may result in a hypernature in which we may grow our houses.[4]

As a historian, Tafuri had (thankfully) little to say about design itself, only about its makers, products, and their purported meaning. But since it is of fundamental importance, I will, under the rubric of architecture reconsidered, well out of Tafuri's sight, explore the underpinnings and processes of the design activity (Herbert Simon) and suggest that we should view the activity as a complex design machine. Part of my escape from Tafuri lies in the darkness and obscurity of the architectural object—a move away from its petrified history toward the fleeting relations with its users and interpreters.

The role of the enlightened architect, outlined by Tafuri as "the ideologist of the city" using "form as the tool" to persuade the public that modernist planning can withstand the hit-or-miss market forces of modern urban organization, has been radically reconstituted. This is very frustrating to modern reflective architects, who see themselves as unwilling instruments of capital without influence on urban organization. Less reflective architects seem equally frustrated because they blame themselves for these same facts. Emasculated and blinded, architects have reached an impasse, and the remedy is not readily apparent. It seems obvious, however, that the role of the architect as the privileged (albeit tragic) hero is defunct because so few are able to play it.

Furthermore there is no longer time or room for what Tafuri called "the free contemplation of our destiny." The metropolis that will soon be absorbed into an all-encompassing *cordon urbain* (urban barrier) will render us all riders, since the driving has been left to an increasingly global market. The demise of the city has erased the borders between city, suburb, and hinterland to form this huge barrier that is sometimes a metropolis and always part of a vast Terrapolis, a world urbanism. The echo of *cordon sanitaire* (a sanitary barrier to protect a city from the plague) is intentional, for the significance of world urbanism is not that it is everywhere, as in a global city, but that in its dominance it delimits and forecloses other alternatives for habitation. Perplexingly, we seem no longer able to "think globally and act locally," because the global and the local are so intertwined that they have become synthetic and inseparable. The alternating wisdom and foolishness of the many will drive us all, although as individual members of a collective we are paradoxically all in the driver's seat. To navigate in this complexity, the new architect need no longer be right (as in ideologically correct), only good.

Tafuri saw both expressionism and its "exasperated objects" and "the destruction of the object" by the Neue Sachlichkeit as desperate attempts to combat the all-engulfing force of the metropolis. His solution was a political and socioeconomic revolution. Yet his analysis, in which he saw the weakness of formfulness and silence as almost equally futile (he preferred silence), points out the futility of seeing form alone. Only in the mind of the architect does form stand alone; in life it is always motivated by use and thought. A willing interlocutor can rescue exasperated and silenced form. These touch on the subjects of the dwellers and their liberty, concerns that are significantly absent from Tafuri's discourse, since they are resolved by his ideology. As I claim, under the rubric of *doublespace,* interpretation—thought—and associated action can free most dwellers from various built ideologies. But this is after Tafuri.

Tafuri's realization that the geometry of the urban plan needed no correspondence in the form of single buildings seems graphically played out in the modern metropolis. But how correct is this observation? The uncoupling of form and infrastructure is consequential on the scale of an individual building and on the scale of city form, but once agglomerated into vast tracks of similar buildings, (suburban) form again begins to shape the metropolis. It is asinine to suggest that the single-family house and its lot, agglomerated, have no consequence for urban form. They are the very cause of our daily commute. These agglomerations, or megaforms, are hard to visualize despite their molecular regimentation (house, lot, and street) because their horizons, their coherence as objects, are fuzzy and disjointed. The sorry news for architects is that the heroes of these consequential megaforms are the Levitts, the Eichlers, and more recently U.S. Homes, and thousands of lesser-known developers and builders who continue to house us.

The decline of the ideological importance of modern architecture as expressed in urban organization is in part the result of the architect's profound isolation from capitalist development. Passive respondents to the vagaries of development, architects are extremely reluctant to join forces ideologically with the undeniable power and productivity of the system in which we are all immersed. The division of labor between architects and developers, designers and builders, thinkers and doers seems ironclad. Furthermore and less agreed upon, architects have failed their potential clients. In the mesmerizing light of the heroic, design architects have been trained to serve the very few, as reflected in the total belief in customization (at a high price) and the uniqueness of each project. The realization, or better the acknowledgment, that all architectural projects are too complex for any one person is not yet accepted by the heroes and their clients. Only a not-so-quiet revolution of the thousands of architects that actually make all the projects possible will change this situation.

The roots of the heroic attitude are deep and ancient. Palladio and Alberti come to mind. Architecture schools are another key perpetrator of this attitude. Education in which innovation, speculation, fantasy, form, and design take the front seat represents failure. Not because design is unimportant, but because design has been profoundly separated from marketing, client relations, and business practices. Binary thinking—division of labor—has so fully permeated the academy that any attempt to put innovation into practice has failed. Thousands of spectacular houses for artists, philosophers, and pile drivers have been presented in as many final juries, without any attempt to show how such projects could be implemented—just in case one such client should appear in the future architect's office. Combine this with the lone-hero attitude embedded in design education and we have the recipe for neurosis if not professional catastrophe.

Instead, architectural educators should promote teamwork and choose the design of authorless objects as their fundamental preoccupation, combined with the integration of design and practice. With time, architects will see how their relevance to the metropolis will be reinvigorated. There is much to learn from industrial design practices and design marketing and distribution. The premise of architectural production as teamwork does not prohibit individuals from playing the role of heroes in their practice. However, before we can rethink curriculum we must rethink the metropolis.

In Piranesi's *Campo Marzio* the "struggle between architecture and city . . . assumes epic tone," according to Tafuri, prefiguring the current "excesses" of the metropolis, excesses made apparent in the lack of structure, the endless repetitions, and the surplus of formalities that seem to speak of nothing but the form itself: "A universe of empty signs is a place of total disorder."[5]

In Piranesi's etchings of the *Carceri d'invenzione,* Tafuri saw the building as an infinite space lacking the horizon and figure that belonged to the old city and its architecture. "What has been destroyed is the center of that space," and what is left is an immeasurable collective form. "Liberated and condemned at the same time," human collectivity "by its own reason" is encased in a "global, voluntary alienation,"[6] Simmel's *Entortung.* Consequently, Piranesi was warning us, or predicting, that the new urban organization was the total "eclipse of form." According to Tafuri, no one seemed to have noticed the collapse of collective meaning, while Tafuri saw two opposing but productive views emerge: "those who search into the very bowels of reality in order to know and assimilate its values and wretchedness; and those who desire to go beyond reality, who want to construct *ex novo* new realties, new values, and new public symbols."[7]

This is the difference that divides the realists from the utopians: "Monet from Cézanne, Munch from Braque, Raoul Hausmann from Mondrian, Häring from Mies, or Rauschenberg from Vasarely."[8] And we could extend these juxtapositions to current heroes/heroines: Koolhaas from Eisenman, Piano from Gehry, SOM from Hejduk, Graves from Frank Lloyd Wright, Venturi/Scott Brown from Paul Rudolph. As always, binary thinking breaks apart and dissolves the purported differences, particularly when the pairings are close to home. Again we encounter the absolutism of the binary. Again, Tafuri found a way out. Significantly for my argument and surreptitiously, he took us across the ocean to L'Enfant's plan for Washington and the many plans and projects by Thomas Jefferson, president and architect of white America par excellence. The third way.

In Jefferson, Tafuri saw a powerful organizer of culture (a true architect), one who constructs the new democratic culture of the United States with the (empty) signs of European culture. But Jefferson's was a conception based on agrarian and antiurban politics that stood in stark contrast to Alexander Hamilton's pragmatic pursuit of "accelerated development of American financial and industrial capital."[9] Jefferson's fear of the potential authoritarian power of capital convinced him of the dangers of the city, and he remained "faithful to a democracy arrested at the level of a utopia."[10] Tafuri brilliantly recognized the Jeffersonian inheritance that still haunts many American intellectuals and politicians—acknowledgment of their system's democratic foundations but opposition to its concrete manifestations, producing the all too prevalent "ambiguous conscience" that I found in myself: a dilemma in which an urban configuration (say in all its market-driven formlessness) is acknowledged as basically democratic but somehow the form it takes is not right, even though the right form is not possible because too utopian. The consequence is ambiguity, uneasiness, and a sense of failure, and the architect feels that he or she is somehow at fault. Of course, in my own case, this was before Houston.

Here the suburban metropolis, of which Houston is a prime example, contains elements, attitudes, and practices of the individual impulse—Hamilton's pragmatism—side by side with the social good—Jefferson's utopia. Neither of these desires is fully synthesized or completely digested. This manifested ambiguity, this flux, this incompleteness mysteriously releases me from my ambiguous conscience because I see complexity, movement, energy, potential, even hope in their explicit contradiction. It is as if the gap between the two desires leaves room for a future that is ours to make, a future that is graphically emblematized by the holes in the urban tissue in all examples of the suburban metropolis, the Holey Plane. The danger of one desire smothering another is tempered by the contradicting gap. Thus, the potential alienation and extreme individualism of Houston is contradicted by one thousand neighborhood organizations, one hundred twenty-three high school bands, six hundred meetings of faith, and by the cultures of a multitude of ethnicities. And the three-hundred-mile freeway system is contradicted by a million mature trees.

Finally after some twenty years Tafuri is behind me. The assertiveness of my proposition in this book reflects my new-won freedom, since it allows me to rethink the metropolis, to reconsider architecture and the role of the architect, and euphorically, at last, to find a new frontier for further architectural deliberations and actions.

After Tafuri's enigmatic smile at our last meeting, he continued his walk across the piazza in front of the Pantheon in Rome, without even looking up at the temple. This is meaningful to me since the Pantheon and its hollow wall, its doublespace, are examples of the built resistance to all forms of ideology. At the Pantheon my own metropolitan consciousness found its agent in the wanderer, later to emerge as the *drifter on the superhighway*. His peripatetic wanderings and roving eyes began their formation under the tutelage of Walter Benjamin, who in his *Berliner Chronik* described his own development of a panoramic view. He wrote of lying in bed as a child and hearing and "seeing" his parents and their guests: "But is not this, too, the city: the strip of light under the bedroom door on evenings when we were *entertaining*."[11] The formation of the metropolitan consciousness is essential to my project. Without the acknowledgment of the wanderer's subjectivity, his point of view, I would never have discovered the potentials of the metropolis. My story begins here.

I can no longer rely on Tafuri the master analyst/synthesizer, on his assured analysis, on his unbending ideological stance, on our tragic destiny. Houston, like Los Angeles, Taipei, and Randstadt Holland, is open, in process, in the making. Their fate is not necessarily sealed. We must take charge of our new-won freedom, displace our ambiguous conscience, and help forge the complexity of forces and desires coursing through the avenues of the metropolis. We must engage the Open City—*la città aperta*. Our enthusiasm for speed and change must be tempered. And the metropolis's spatial flows (Castells) must be manipulated, shaped, and rerouted. Global euphoria must be coupled with local energies. Although our IQs may be improving, we still eat, sleep, and die housed in the same vulnerable body saddled with the same, often poorly expressed, insatiable desire for love, friendship, and community.

The Wanderer, Authority, and Doublespace

The Straying Gaze

The very idea of carving an armored car out of stone smacks of a certain psychological acceleration, of the sculptor being a bit ahead of his time. As far as I know, this is the only monument to a man on an armored car that exists in the world. In this respect alone, it is a symbol of a new society. The old society used to be presented by men on horseback.

—Joseph Brodsky, describing a statue of Lenin standing on top of an armored car in front of former Leningrad's Finland Station, in "A Guide to a Renamed City," in *Less Than One: Selected Essays*

The wanderer's eyes stray from the center—from Lenin's statue to the armored car. It may be curiosity, shame, boredom, even a kind of laziness that makes the gaze waver and shift its focus to the margin. Like a hand before the eyes, this is a view that favors the horizon over the center.

At this margin, fused here at Finland Station, are Lenin's vehicle and the customary base. The traditional equestrian has been replaced by a pedestrian, standing on an armored car (in implied motion) that in turn replaces the fixity of the customary base, the miniature version of the same base that sets up the tripartite facade of the classical Renaissance palazzo, versions of which hover not far from here. By implication, the anthropomorphic trace slips across the margins from horse to armored car, from the old to the new society, from the lofty equestrian hero to the man of the street,[12] from nobility to working class, from the statue to the palazzo, whose monumentality and expression of authority Georges Bataille linked to the prison—a monumentality which, as with the Bastille, would eventually be attacked by the storming mob of the street, the stonemasons, the bronze casters, the grooms, and the crews of the armored cars. Let us follow the *dérive* (drift) of the straying gaze. Radically peripatetic, let's move from city to city, from revolution to revolution, by the mob and by the petrified armored car that left its base in the dust (and recently its rider too). Let's trade Leningrad and Paris for Rome, and Lenin and his revolution for Trajan and his column, or better for his successor Hadrian and his Pantheon. Here too, the foundations will shift.

The straying gaze needs its centers as parasites require hosts. At the Pantheon we can establish at least three, apart from the perspective of strict architectural history that forms the basis for the entire discussion.[13] The first is drawn by Michel Serres and his stones momentarily at rest in the foundations of Rome, the second by Michel Foucault and his all-seeing eye forcing us, confined to the interior of the building, to confess, and the third by Denis Hollier in his interpretation of Georges Bataille, whose man in the piazza is squashed by the sheer monumentality of the building.

The perspectives are not entirely comparable, but serve as strategic positions in this text. Serres's is historical and poetic and serves as the foundation for my argument. The two others are recto and verso of the same coin, fixed points of the stage on which the primary plot of this text is acted out. Foucault and Hollier will set the rules for the action, while Serres will assist in the escape. As "the peasant gives the land a landscape,"[14] these nuclei of steady gazes will help to construct a set of positions in and around the ancient monument, positions that curve, shape, and delimit our conceptual geography. The faint outline of a space appears between them—a lacuna—a lunar lake that in its solid darkness is hard pressed to reveal its secrets.

Stones at Rest

Geometry has to make itself stone before the word can make itself flesh. . . . The object apprehended by Galileo required two worlds, or rather two spaces and one time. The incandescent space of geometry and the dark world of opaque mass. Nothing is so easy as to understand the first—it is there only to understand and be understood; nothing is so easy to hear as the word—it is there to be heard; but nothing so obscure as the second—nothing so difficult to conceive as the body, flesh or stone, nothing so hard to hear as the sound that escapes from it; nothing is so difficult as to know how it receives and envelops light.
—Michel Serres, *Rome: The Book of Foundations*

Geometry versus Stone

Geometrically speaking (which historians have done well), the Pantheon is a sphere, a miniature universe, a heaven on earth—a mental structure to be kept in one's head for memory's sake, precise, clear, and there to be heard. On the other hand, behind its immediate surface the Pantheon is dark, thick, and formidable in its ambiguity. The Pantheon as material, as stone, as the other space, or even specifically as bricks, rocks, mortar, and Roman concrete, will not break its silence. To apprehend it briefly via the anthropometric trace, it is a giant black skull, towering and wide, filling now in a world of Lilliputians one end of a small piazza. It and the sculpture of Trajan on its priapic column are considered to be the two most spectacular Roman monuments. How and why they have survived is ambiguous at best:

> Barbarians demolish buildings in order to bring the stone back to its function as projectile: wisdom builds in order to immobilize stone to appease hatred, to protect. Why do you think we have walls, towns, and temples, when we could sleep under the stars and prostrate ourselves before the horizon? We have only built to settle stones, which could otherwise fly continually in our midst. The builder's plans barely count: the architectonic ideal exists only for representation—the point is that projectiles come to rest.[15]

Rome as represented by the Pantheon is a quarry of weapons, dormant, petrified, and opaque. As such, the Pantheon is a perfect symbol of Rome, because it is as if this lowbrow city had escaped all of the academic contemplation that is associated with the city: "Science never appeared in Rome, nor did geometry or logic: never anything but politics."[16] Imported for the convenience of politics (and warfare), the geometry of the half-circle that haunts the outer cupola and inner room (and our giant black skull) was for the Romans only a way to get to the projectiles—to the object—and this suits us fine. The difference between the geometry of the ideal sphere that lingers in the Pantheon and the bordering outer geometry of the ideal Roman city—the checkerboard of the encampment—is just a line. The built difference between the spherical interior of the inner space of the temple, the outer skull, and the twisting fabric of the street is a gap filled by the opaque mass of material. This suits us fine too, because it is into this darkness that we will eventually stray.

Gray versus Black

As our first position, this fabric of stone must be held right here, because even as an arsenal of projectiles it becomes too metaphoric: the rocks and bricks will probably never fly again. The Pantheon's weakness as an assembly of projectiles is already too theoretical. In fact, *all referentiality must be held back* in order for us to retain the Pantheon's status as an opaque black mass. It may well be that we should refer to it as *gray* mass, recalling Foucault's speculation on painting:

> It is in vain that we say what we see; what we see never resides in what we say. And it is in vain that we attempt to show, by the use of images, metaphors, or similes, what we are saying; the space where they achieve their splendor is not that deployed by our eyes. . . . But if one wishes to keep the relation of language to vision open, if one wishes to treat their incompatibility as a starting-point for speech instead of as an obstacle to be avoided, so as to stay as close as possible to both, then one must erase these proper names and preserve the infinity of the task. It is perhaps through the medium of this gray, anonymous language, always over-meticulous and repetitive because too broad, that the painting may, little by little, release its illuminations.[17]

Simply put, the monument is a pile of rocks, stacked to be sure, and seen too close to reveal their horizon. And the light is bleak—just after daybreak. For now the insights are kept oblique. Here at degree zero, the wanderer's eyes remain in chiaroscuro.

The Eye in the Center

Insideoutside

It rained the day the wanderer first came to realize the Pantheon's ambiguous status as "inside." A group of children danced in a circle, their faces upturned to catch the rain that in a fine mist fell from the great oculus in the sky. They were outside inside. Now the spherical interior wall becomes a facade. This may have been the ultimate intention of Nolli's map of Rome that includes in the rendition of the city with its streets and piazzas the interiors of the monuments, while the rest of the city with its dwellings and its work spaces is drawn as opaque and impenetrable. It is the bright light of the public world and the darkness of the private, Hannah Arendt's Greek *polis*. The purpose of this duality was "to render accessible to a multitude of men the inspection of a small number of objects: this was the problem to which the architecture of temples, theatres and circuses responded."[18] When the wanderer joins his fellow tourists with their guides, maps, and incessant picture-taking, it is the opposite pole that comes to mind: "to procure for a small number of people, or even for a single individual, the instantaneous view of a great multitude."[19] Thus it is Foucault's reading of Bentham's Panopticon that comes to mind—architecture as a prison in which all space is controlled interior space. In fact, public space has disappeared in favor of social space. Although the Pantheon is of antiquity and therefore, according to Foucault, rendered to serve the spectacle, the spectacle has also disappeared. The architectural skull is left behind, but the world has changed, and radically. As Foucault writes, "We are much less Greek than we believe. We are neither in the amphitheatre, nor on the stage, but in the panoptic machine, invested by its effects of power, which we bring ourselves since we are part of its mechanism."[20]

Surveillance

Bentham's Panopticon in its idealized form consists of two concentric spaces, with "an annular building" at the periphery and a tower at the center. The tower is fitted with windows, as are the cells in the peripheral part of the building. The guards occupying the tower have the prisoners in full view. The building is thus fully transparent, but once the guards cannot be seen by the prisoners the "architectural apparatus" can sustain "the power relation independent of the person who exercises it, in short, that the inmates [are] caught up in a power situation of which they are themselves the bearers."[21]

The Pantheon, caught in this Panoptic gaze, transforms the body of the emperor into light. The great oculus, rain or shine, throws light—diffuse (when overcast) or focused and columnar (when sunny)—across the space. Focused, the searchlight wanders across the warped surfaces. As in a theater set, the cells are rendered in *trompe-l'oeil* from niches and coffers. Since the light never occupies the center, not even at the height of summer, there is no way to confuse oneself with the geometrical axis of the oculus and the center of the floor plan—the star, or the Celtic diagram, as Serres would describe it. The wanderer remains displaced, while the light is searching for him. If the wanderer is Hadrian, is this column of light Trajan? It must be so, since the light fathers the space.

Panoptically speaking, the Pantheon is post-Panoptic. The central tower, in which anyone may come and exercise "the functions of surveillance," has been removed and replaced by the giant searchlight, the reminder of the father. From Foucault's perspective, the wanderer is here "alone" with his fellow tourists under the auspices of generalized surveillance. The incessant urge to photograph, the urge to listen to the platitudes of tour guides, the obsessive reading of packaged history in guidebooks: all neglect to "use" the building, or even just look at it, in the way children once did. Touching is prohibited. This is the manifestation of "the new physics of power . . . which has its maximum intensity not in the person of the king, but in the bodies that can be individualized by these relations"[22] in the generalized function of tourist behavior. This disciplinary mechanism becomes even more apparent when the column of light is diffused and it rains.

The Hollow

There is an escape. Although authorities must sanction the departure, the wanderer can momentarily steal away from the crowd: the spherical wall, with its interior facade overlooking the space we know as the Pantheon, is partially hollow. In fact, it can be occupied.

The disciplinary subject of the great space has a double that, through the crevices, may observe the *Doppelgänger's* attempt to avoid the light. The Panoptic theater has been turned inside out. The observer has become the observed. Yet, as we shall see later, this observer has no power, unless being close to the formal meaning of the monument endows this marginal subject with a certain wisdom.

The Face of Power

Bataille's prison derives from an ostentatious, spectacular architecture, an architecture to be seen; whereas Foucault's prison is the embodiment of an architecture that sees, observes, and spies, a vigilant architecture. Bataille's architecture—convex, frontal, extrovert—an architecture that is externally imposing, shares practically no element with that of Foucault, with its insinuating concavity that surrounds, frames, contains, and confines for therapeutic or disciplinary ends. Both are equally effective, but one works because it draws attention to itself and the other because it does not. One represses (imposes silence); the other expresses (makes one talk).

—Denis Hollier, *Against Architecture: The Writings of Georges Bataille*

The Skull

The forest of the giant portico's columns rushes by; released, the wanderer stumbles out in the blinding light of the piazza. Turning around, he faces the outer monument for the second time.

"Convex, frontal, extrovert": the skull of the Pantheon, with its grin of columns, dominates his space. He stands in silence. Drifting, his gaze wanders to the bent horizon of the skull; the space between it and its jagged but rectilinear surround forms a blue shape, a lake between two worlds, one domestic, snug, and warm, the other imposing, broad, and stifling.

The wanderer's eyes oscillate from the majestic portico to the bent side elevations that, in their sober mural economy, curve themselves and, with the stepped cupola, create an infinite bow to the sky. Tensile and taut, the Pantheon bulges like a sail whose ragged, pockmarked, and petrified surface anchors it to the geology below.

Auguste Rodin spoke of "l'exagération des formes," in which the exaggeration exploded from within the stone to rush toward the surface. This allowed Rodin to amplify a torso or limb so that the rest of the body would be rendered unnecessary. The fragment became the whole. The giant skull of Hadrian bulges with an explosive inner power that, despite the wear of time, the loss of meaning, its status as tourist trap, and clouds of sulfuric acid, still exaggerates.

Domination and Transgression

Bataille states, "Thus great monuments are erected like dikes, opposing the logic and majesty of authority against all disturbing elements: it is in the form of the cathedral or palace that Church or State speaks to the multitudes and imposes silence upon them."[23] As Hollier suggests, Bataille sees architecture not just as an image of social order, but as instrumental in imposing the order: "From being a simple symbol it has become master."[24] There is an anthropomorphic sleight of hand at work here—the monument becomes a sentry, a human form. This is of particular interest, because the order the Pantheon imposes on our wanderer—now

Bataille's subject—is all there is. The skull is empty; its brain is gone.

The Pantheon is what the Italian architectural theorist Aldo Rossi calls "a pathological permanence": it is a museum of itself.[25] Bataille may approve of this pathology, and see it as an internal transgression, as the improbable putrefaction of the already petrified. For Bataille, argues Hollier, architecture is but the skeleton, the structure of human form: "Architecture retains of man only what death has no hold on."[26] The Pantheon, because of its internal demise—the collapse of its center—is no longer reproducible. Once pollution has done its devastating job, there will be no more Pantheons.

Consequently, once the wanderer gets beyond the imposing skull, the Pantheon reveals a truth: it is a corpse. The imposing power that it emanates is empty, symbolic. The intention of the rendering of Bataille's position, however, is to keep the subject imprisoned at the origin of his fixed gaze. The Pantheon is "grouping servile multitudes" and, in its shadow, "imposing admiration and astonishment, order and constraint."[27] "Architecture," writes Hollier, "does not express the soul of societies but rather smothers it."[28] It is this suffocating dimension of architecture that will eventually fuel our wanderer's trespass.

In Bataille's view, architecture is a complex villain, even if it is static and stubbornly consistent. Standing somewhere between monkeys, men, and mathematics, architecture as an armature of domination is hard to tackle precisely because it is so easily confused with our own body. When we attack architecture, we attack man.

"If the prison is the generic form of architecture this is primarily because man's own form is his first prison," Hollier writes. In Bataille's view, writes Hollier, "the only way to escape the architectural chain gang is to escape his form, to lose his head."[29]

The Pantheon seems again to reveal a certain internal weakness, a second transgression. Hadrian has managed the impossible: he escapes the prison by leaving his skull behind (to paraphrase Bataille). The writing on the pediment of the portico (visible from the wanderer's position in the piazza), "Agrippa built this," may then be Hadrian's last joke: leaving his skull with the incorrect address.[30] With the Pantheon severed from its body, untraceable, both the father standing on his column and his decapitated son fade away.

The Doublespace

Lacuna

Three positions—the opaque mass of the built substance and two prisons (one concave, the other convex)—are all cradled in the official history of the monument. As conceptual dominions, however, they do not fully map out the Pantheon. Much like the lines in a value engineer's graph, they leave a problem space, an uncharted territory—a lacuna (and potentially others that I cannot see). In the starkness of the real, this is particularly obvious: even a novice knows that when he passes from one prison to the other there is a gap.

Our wanderer first encounters the gap when he rushes through the portico, moving between the two prisons. This is a prime example of Benjamin's "distracted perception."[31] The wanderer does not see the forest of columns, not just for the columns but for the pull of the space beyond, be it the outside or the inside. Only if he stops will the lacuna with the immense stillness of a petrified forest immerse him. The architectural figure of the portico is here invisible. What is offered is only the insistent physical presence of the repeated shaped and stacked stone disks, the lowered light, the sudden cool, the draft between inside and outside across his face and bared wrists.

Once inside, the second encounter comes when the wanderer's eyes drift from the candles and saints to linger in the niches, imprints that begin to hint at the actual nature of the wall. At first solid and continuous, with the invasion of the indentations the wall becomes porous, permeable, and partially transparent. In fact, the entire structure is made apparent with the eight huge pylons that form the footprint of the immense half-sphere above. The formerly continuous wall is now made up of what Goethe, in speaking of Palladian villas, called the "contradiction" between surface and column. This contradiction stalls, if briefly, the onslaught of representation—of speech—to expose the writing of the wall. The wanderer has his third and ultimate encounter with the gap when he discovers that the wall between the pylons is hollow and occupiable.

Intra Muros

Hollier refers repeatedly to a "gap" when he compares Foucault and Bataille, and also when he compares the slaughterhouse and the museum. These gaps are conceptual and actual distances between loci. It is their status as voids that is significant, because the subtle and insidious connection between the loci is intramural. It is genetically inscribed. Bataille's view of the slaughterhouse and the museum has resonance in the Pantheon too. As Serres describes, much blood was spilled, even among brothers, during the foundation of Rome. Some of it was certainly spilled in and around the foundations of Pantheon, and now it is a museum. Hollier writes, "The slaughterhouses are the negative pole, the generator of repulsion, the centrifuge. . . . Museums, the pole of attraction, are centripetal. But within the heart of one the other is hidden."[32] Quoting Bataille, Hollier concludes: "The origin of the modern museum would thus be linked to the development of the guillotine."[33] The distance between the slaughterhouse on the periphery of the city and the museum at the center is essential in maintaining their difference because of their similarity. This similarity is a symmetry without likeness. As prisons, the exterior and interior Pantheons are also symmetries without likeness, but as unified built substance their story is more complex.

The Pantheon-as-severed-head is a telling emblem of the veritable slaughterhouse that lies at the foundation of Serres's Rome. The gap in the Pantheon's wall is neither sheer distance nor is it a vacuum; like a catacomb it is the secret refuge between the two surrounds and forms, but blood has seeped in here as well. The inner gap is the mold of the two outsides—it is a space of transformation.

The void between Bataille's slaughterhouse and museum remains a simple geometrical distance: like that between day and night, or like the single shadow cast by a single light. Our gap is much more complex: the built in-between is not completely independent of outside or inside. A built distance, the gap is a quasi-space, a space in between wall and space.

In reference to our gap, the status of Serres's pile of rocks is more obscure than that of the prisons. The built material—the bricks, the rocks, and the Roman concrete in the Pantheon's case—make up, to borrow Rossi's term, the *fabbrica*,[34] but since there is a physical gap in this *fabbrica* it is not just solid material: the gap is a space, however narrow, made up of enclosed air surrounded by material. The tear in the descriptive-conceptual tissue is thus in the Pantheon both a gap and a place, but more important it is a locus of transit, like a tunnel between two worlds. An atmosphere prevails here: the compressed air of the interior's interior, light from both inside and outside transformed by the double wall to mix new light that in turn does not light very well, and sound that reverberates rather than communicates. This locus, like a peripheral other, repeats and doubles both the outer and inner monument, but lies outside the focus of what Norman Bryson calls "the menacing gaze."[35]

Le Regard—The Gaze

The genealogy of the disturbed and disturbing gaze in modern French thinking is a large and complex subject, and indeed is an essential ingredient of both Foucault's and Bataille's conceptions of their prisons. Bryson's essay "The Gaze in the Expanded Field" attempts to investigate "where the modern subject resides." This is important for architecture because the architect always assumes a subject, more or less consciously, for a building—the architect's homunculus. In turn the building as institution produces a subject—Foucault's and Bataille's subject—that may not necessarily coincide with the assumed subject. Third, the building may also have its own subject that, like a phantom, resides in the building's very material, what we could call a formal subject—Serres's and architecture's subject. Modern life attempts to spin all subjects away from their natural center, which produces an additional decentered subject.

Bryson argues that in Jean-Paul Sartre and Jacques Lacan, despite their desire to decenter the subject, the "line of thinking remains held within a conceptual enclosure where vision is still theorized from the standpoint of a subject placed at the center of the world."[36] This can also be said of Foucault and Bataille vis-à-vis architecture as a prison. Rather than following Bryson's path to complete decenteredness or "nothingness" in the "expanded field" of Eastern philosophy, however, I shall enter into the gap.

The Double Wall

If we imagine the wanderer, now climbing stairs inside the wall of the Pantheon, we can assume that it is quite dark, and that kinesthetic sensations join with vision to aid his advancement.[37] If he ascends clockwise through the wall, its bulging convexity will be sensed by his right hand—a microcosmic "same" in Bataille's view, though the rough and gently curving surface must be more akin to a giant vessel than to a prison. The left hand will touch and feel the outer surface, the concave other. Unless our climber is claustrophobic, it is not "surveillance" that must come to mind but materiality on the one hand and corporeality on the other.

Here in the gap of the wall, the two outer gazes are tamed, disrupted, and displaced by the inner calm of the wall. This inner world has momentarily blinded all menacing gazes. The subject has been taken out of his obsessive self-enclosure to become one with the building's own enclosure. He has been decentered, moved out of the spectacle of the gaze of either prison. He has not been dumped in the darkness of Serres's pile of rocks, however, but into a narrow slot of faint light that leads him to the top of the world. He has also been returned to his body. But this is not an "untroubled place of acrobatic grace and perceptual accord between subject-world and object-world,"[38] nor is it the place for Jacques Derrida's "spaced out" subject, who in some delirious state avoids all attempts by architecture to produce its subject. This is only a momentary escape, a place of readjustment, reflection, and distance—architecture's catacomb. This gap is a perspective other than that of the prison. It is another position, another place—possibly the only one in the Pantheon with a certain conceptual stillness. At least for the moment.

The gap is a place away from the insistent shadows of the various menacing figures, a place whose weight and value are in its material and its lack of reflective visual distance. A subject is produced here, but it is architecture's subject rather than the institution's or the critic's. Although this place may have a certain conceptual vacuity, its status is slippery and so is its subject.

Architecture

In *The Life of Forms in Art,* Henri Focillon gives us an important clue from whence we might project this subject. Like Foucault, Focillon believed that architecture produces a subject, and in fact he maintains that entire styles do, *en bloc*: "Gothic art, as a landscape, created a France and a French humanity that no one could foresee: outlines of the horizon, silhouettes of cities—a poetry, in short, that arose from Gothic art, and not from geology or from Capetian institutions."[39] Focillon's work offers a very different take on architecture's role. Here there is no menacing gaze, but not because his is the view of an apolitical art historian; rather, a different status is given to form itself, and to its production. He writes: "Form has a meaning—but it is a meaning entirely its own, a personal and specific value that must not be confused with the attributes we impose on it."[40] Meanings such as those Foucault and Bataille associate with architecture come and go. Interpretations are both "unstable and insecure. As old meanings are broken down and obliterated, new meanings attach themselves to form."[41]

The form of the Pantheon remains the same, and so does its own "personal and specific value." The narrow path that loops through the Pantheon's wall is as close as we can come to the actual construction of the monument. In the innards, the arduous task of making such an immense structure reveals itself, unadorned—pedantically, as it were. Inside out, the microcosm of the two outer monuments—the inner cave and the outer skull—appears at the end of the body at its fingertips rather than at the end of a panoramic and "disturbed" gaze. Inside the wall, this reversal of inside and outside brings this interspace close to the status of a mold, like the mold from which the bronze statue of Lenin sprang, or the pink rubbery mold that the dentist takes of a patient's teeth. Mysteriously separate, peripheral, and humble, molds are yet the font from which the object arises. As a mold, the inner world of the Pantheon is real, gritty, and even dusty when it unashamedly reveals itself to our wanderer's touch. Form's "extraordinary vigor" (Rodin's exaggeration) stems from this inner gap, but form cannot be found here, since it has already exploded to the outer surfaces. It is the calm after the storm, but what about the explosion itself, or its traces?

Flung Ink

In Norman Bryson's example of the achievement of "nothingness," he uses an example of a fifteenth-century Ch'an painting by Jiun depicting the calligraphic sign for "man." In a flung-ink painting, the sign is done with great speed, so that the common stability and secure flow achieved by the deliberately careful movement of the skilled hand is abandoned to the speed of the gesture. This speed, combined with the effect of gravity, allows the ink to break its own surface viscosity. The result is a liquidity and independence of line that threatens the sign's function as exclusively a vehicle of meaning by forcing the sign into a double status: it is both form and figure, each with its independent claim to meaning.[42]

Similarly, the incidental and unkempt intimacy of the interspace (when juxtaposed with the precision and representability of the interior space and the unified power of the sign of the monument on the outside) produces the space from which the architectural subject can be molded. This subject is a formal consciousness. The very act of making and constructing dominates this subject. Inside the wall, the outer form as reflected and the inner form as also reflected are secondary to their own construction. The entire architectural algorithm is exposed, not just its answers or its figures. In contradistinction, the great interior space is made for an idealized observer whose interest is the meaning (a facsimile of the universe) rather than the factuality of the building, the *fabbrica*. The interspace—the mold of both outside and inside—like a gene holds the inscription of the architectural act itself. (Like a bicycle's inner tube, it supports the apparent stability and strength of the outer tire.) I shall call this inner, interspace the "doublespace."

The doublespace is produced, if not with the willfulness of the Ch'an painter, at least outside the view of the Commendatore.[43] He couldn't care less what happens here as long as the building stands up. Consequently, we can be sure that the Roman concrete was flung here with great gusto and speed. Like the broken line of the sign for "man" in the painting described above, the doublespace defies perception as geometrically defined; only fractal geometry would do.

Time Out

The privileged importance given to this insignificant cavity in the Pantheon's wall has a modernist history. When Le Corbusier made the distinction between structure and surface in his walls, the walls were also given a new interiority. This formal manifestation of internal differences led the Italian architect Giuseppe Terragni to separate entire systems of columns and walls in order to produce zones of in-betweens to which various activities could be assigned. Each zone was given its own vocabulary, clearly distinguished from the rest of the building. The beginning of this internal decomposition has, as the case of the Pantheon proves, been falsely associated with Le Corbusier. To be sure, the Pantheon is not the origin either.

The importance of this territory within the architectural body lies not only in its formal possibilities, but in its formal significance. Differences in architecture are often driven by functional distinctions, but here they are driven by the nature of the form itself. This work is being done on the very vehicle of Focillon's formal meaning.

Architecture, as understood by Bataille and Foucault, "is the expression of every society's being." Hollier writes:

> Architecture represents a religion that it brings alive, a political power that it manifests, an event that it commemorates, etc. Architecture, before any other qualifications, is identical to the space of representation;

it always represents something other than itself from the moment it becomes distinguished from mere building.[44]

The rewriting of the Pantheon attempts to claim an additional territory for architecture in the gap between architecture as representation and architecture as mere building. Simply put, architecture for Hollier and others is a form of speech, while by now it is also a form of writing, in Derrida's sense of the word which reverses the traditional priority of the immediacy of speech over the physicality of writing. The doublespace, the interspace, the time-out space is the other side of the coin of architecture, like "the hinge" as the common term for "articulation and difference" in *Of Grammatology*.[45] The articulation of the doublespace is the difference. This space is not dominated by the fixed gaze but by the straying gaze, and because the stage is dimly lit, the weaker senses are allowed their much deserved handicap. (Vision has dominated architecture, as speech has writing.) If this is the acknowledgment of a certain autonomy of architecture, then, to paraphrase Norman Mailer, "architecture's empty skull may have found its brain."

A New Map

The "acknowledgment of a certain autonomy" could be understood as an attempt to return to an earlier and more dogmatic time, but it is in fact the opposite in more than one way. The tactic used to escape the state and its disciplinary mechanisms belongs in the still obscure realm of what Machiavelli called *virtù* or more generally "the thinking of the public square." In the Pantheon the wanderer, emerging from the mass in the piazza in front, escapes momentarily into the chiaroscuro of the doublespace, and there joins, out of sight, seamlessly with this space that thanks to its relative autonomy becomes the other in a Dionysian union.

What, specifically, is the threat to the bond between the architectural object and its other—the architect and, alas, the man in the street? The threat may neither be Serres's mob demolishing the Pantheon, chasing away its devotees with the building material as projectiles, nor Foucault's disciplinary power grid, nor even Bataille's hegemony of the state that forces architecture to be mere representation. On the one hand, Serres's proposition is surpassed by far more efficient ways of arming the mob, and on the other hand, the "paranoias" of Foucault and Bataille are rendered finite and limited because their extent has been severed by the momentary autonomy—by the doublespace—"the gap in the garment," as Barthes wrote in another context.[46] And perhaps more fundamentally, discipline and state are limited by their affiliation to *either* the interior or the exterior realm, which is particularly ineffective in a world in which there is no longer an easy distinction between the two—even Nolli would have difficulties drawing the map.

The threat is now far more sinister, since the three previous threats still had some blind spots in which the subject could work and hide and remain in his reverie while the object was overlooked. The threat is more violent and more random in its specific attacks, but it is also more pervasive in that it is all-enclosing. Tentatively such a culprit is best illustrated by the pollution that is slowly attacking the Pantheon's beautiful horizon (and city dwellers, aficionados, and members of the mob alike). Pollution of course solicits yawns in some quarters and hysterical fervor in others, so we must delve beyond pollution's common culprits—the automobile, the factory, and belching cows—to the market system, and to its harshest expression—the ubiquitous bottom line—drawn now not only across Reagan's former Free World but even across Albania and the biggest market of all, China. The curious nature of the bottom line is that it pops out of all the pores of the city, leaking from the very gaps that gave us respite. Out of this frenzied drift the vague contours of a new map emerge. Its constituent parts are momentary coalitions between subjects and objects rather than the neat separations between the actors and the fixed receptacles and channels of the past. The new coalitions collide seemingly at random. At best the events leave traces, imprints, compressions, dents, flecks, flickers, and flows, all evading the marks of common cartography yet taking shape. Partially invisible to the naked eye, not unlike toxic clouds, these new shapes have come to invade the wanderer—now a metropolitan subject—to give the architectural object a new status and the dweller and the architect new roles. To face this ultimate challenge, the subject reconstituted to all his senses in the doublespace must, vis-à-vis his desired object, add strategy to his tactics—stray as it were from his position in the public square. Add a measure of speed. Fumbling in the darkness of the doublespace will not do. He must take the other position of Machiavelli's Prince, now far above the square in the castle. Our wanderer may conceptually have to move as fast as capital but also so fast that he appears to stand still, allowing the subject to synthesize with Focillon's animated object, without losing their respective autonomies. This ultimate commingling sweeps up the stones with the paranoias, racing along surfaces, cutting out beyond the building, thrusting the subject—mind and all his new-won senses—into the vast complex of the metropolis.

II
The Suburban Metropolis

Looking out from below the night sky, the aviator no longer sees cities as solitary light sources struggling against the darkness. Instead homologies of nebulas, here cast on the ground, make up luminous vapors, streaks, zones, and clusters of lights that threaten the supremacy of the darkness they occupy. The metropolitan galaxy has replaced the city as a singularity. The density of this galaxy varies radically, and somewhere in the middle of the spectrum from bright to faint lies the suburban metropolis.

Stim and Dross: Rethinking the Metropolis

stim

  As in *stimulation* (William Gibson in *Mona Lisa Overdrive*),
  Stimme: voice, *Stimmung*: ambience

dross

  1. *Waste product* or *impurities* formed on the surface of molten metal during
  smelting.
  2. Worthless *stuff* as opposed to valuables or value. *Dregs.*

rethinking

  Changing one's point of view, finding a new vocabulary.

metropolis

  No definition.

Houston, 28th Floor. At the Window

The sky is as dark as the ground; the stars, piercingly bright like a million astral
specks, have fallen onto the city, rendering all else pitch black. On this light-
studded scrim the stationary lights appear confident, the moving ones, like tracer
bullets, utterly determined, while the pervasive blackness throws everything else
into oblivion. The city's like a giant switchboard, its million points either on or off.

   Behind this almost motionless scene hovers the metropolis. The more I stare at
it, the more it begins to stir.[1] A vast psychophysical map rolls out to fill my window
like Marcel Duchamp's *Large Glass*, cut at midpoint by a bright horizon: a dense
band of lights flickering hysterically, like a great milky way sending myriad distress
signals about its impending demise. Enter the chocolate grinder, the bride, and her
nine bachelors, and yet a third field speedily emerges. Pulsating from below, the
flurry momentarily draws attention from Duchamp's frozen figures to the dynamics
of their interactions, the abrasive motions of work and the throbbing tensions of
sexual strife. Visible patterns in the glass may be few, but the individual points and
their various qualities and constellations are many: cool and warm, some red, some
green, mostly yellow. Closer—or better, in the lower portion of the Glass—the mov-

ing lights easily match the intensity of the far more numerous immobile ones, suggesting the monstrous possibility that none are definitively fixed. All is labile, transient, as if it were only a question of time before all these lit particles would move—billiard balls on a vast table, unless the table is not itself a fluid in motion? Physicists abstract from these flux-fields features such as smoothness, connections to points-particles, and rules of interaction (between sources, sinks, cycles, and flows). "Where space was once Kantian, [embodying] the possibility of separation, it now becomes the fabric which connects all into a whole."[2] Nothing on the plane is stationary, everything is fluid—even the ground itself on which the billiard balls career. The bio-vehicular, electro-commercial, socio-electronic, and optico-ocular metropolis knows no steady state. In a city predominantly constituted by motion and temporalities, space is about deformation and velocity, constantly being carved out in front and abandoned behind. Definitive now the end of the Corbusian promenade, and the Corbusian subject as the gentleman puppet on the architect's string. The post-Corbusian subject emerges as a complex amalgam of Benjamin's *Angelus Novus* ("a storm irresistibly propels him into the future to which his back is turned, while the pile of debris before him grows skyward. This storm . . . we call progress") and an omni-gendered drifter—the wo-man-vehicle—whose subjectivity engulfs the futurist reflections of Duchamp's descending nude (and the subsequent bachelors) and the tuned-out yet wired-in driver cruising along the superhighways of the metropolis.[3]

The European metropolis-without-crowds has skipped westward while radically transforming itself into a new creature, leaner, meaner, and more superficial but harder to catch, at once simpler and less bearable to live in. This shift was prefigured by Robert Smithson in 1972 in an interview with Paul Cummings: "I was also interested in a kind of suburban architecture: plain box buildings, shopping centers, that kind of sprawl. And I think this is what fascinated me in my earlier interest in Rome, just this kind of collection, this junk heap of history. But here we are confronted with a consumer society. I know there is a sentence in *The Monuments of Passaic* where I said, *Hasn't Passaic replaced Rome as the Eternal City?*"[4]

Megashape

Back at my window the palimpsest of a new city flaunts its hypertextuality in black and light. Its mental map of diverse subjectivities rarely operates while one is on foot, a predicament that hints at the possibility of a new visibility, a new field with emergent, unexpected *megashapes* apprehensible but only at vastly different scales of motion.[5] We can expect megashapes to be quite complex. On the one hand we have a megashape such as the zoohemic canopy, constituted by a myriad of trees of varying species, size, and maturity. On the other, we have downtown,[6] which is formed by the tight assembly of skyscrapers. Both shapes rely on repetition, one of many small elements, the other of a fairly small assembly of large elements. Though the two megashapes seem different, both are apprehended through shifts and distortions of scale and speed. Downtown relies less on speed than on distance. Both would require modern mathematics for analytical description. The canopy demands a special kind of attentiveness, since it operates on the periphery of everyday vision. However, once focused on, trees get counted and form with time and repetition a zoohemic appreciation—even the pedestrian gets a sense of the forest. More intriguing, the canopy is understood from within, from the counting of trees, not from the realization of the whole. There are two ways of seeing the canopy, one from within and the other from the perspective of the aerial field (such as the space all across the city viewed from the 28th floor). Radically different, they don't lead to the same appreciation (form?): one is close and intimate, the other cool and distant. This double reading brings downtown and canopy together conceptually, since driving inside downtown may likewise lead to an appreciation of its megashape quite different from the shape gathered from a distant position in the aerial field. There seem, then, to be at least two readings of any megashape, one from inside leading to an appreciation of the algorithm of the shape (or its *taxis*, to borrow from classical thought), and one from outside which leads to an understanding of the whole—the figure (the result of the algorithm, once solved). The inside appreciation may well be the more interesting, because it suggests that a megashape may be imagined through a fragment and thus does not require completion, while the outside view requires the more traditional perspective as well as an apprehension of the whole. The *fieldroom,* for example (simultaneously a field and a room), consists of one actual dimension—the room—and one imaginary or extrapolated dimension—

the field. How we reconstruct or think about downtown's megashape may be similarly developed.

Intention

The task at hand—in a most rudimentary way—is to trace the lineaments of this city. The desire to capture this elusive creature is audacious and presumptuous, offered in the spirit of Reyner Banham whose ruminations on the four ecologies of Los Angeles serve as a constant inspiration,[7] because Houston, most perplexingly (and despite its deeply conservative and isolating tendencies), is a metropolis waiting and poised for the great adventure.

The Plane, the Riders, and Air Space

Houston is a different planet. Here space in the European sense is scarce, even nonexistent. With neither sea nor confining walls to define it, it consists only of a mottled plane to navigate.[8] By turns smooth, undulating, and choppy, this surface medium appears endless—oceanic during a downpour, a periodic, torrential "pouring" that constitutes one of the critical affects of this (en)Gulf(ing) city. Its plane is crude and wild, marked by fissures, vacated space, and bits of untouched plain, aptly described by what Robert Smithson found in New Jersey: "[Passaic] seems full of 'holes' compared to New York City, which seems tightly packed and solid, and those holes . . . are the monumental vacancies that define, without trying, the memory-traces of an abandoned set of futures."[9] Unloved yet naturalistic, this *holey plane* seems more a wilderness than the datum of a man-made city. Dotted by trees and crisscrossed by wo-men-vehicles/roads, it is a surface dominated by a peculiar sense of ongoing struggle: the struggle of economics against nature. Both the trees and machines of this plane emerge as the trail or dross of that struggle. In New York and Paris such a precarious, unstable status is unthinkable. There nature has been defeated, erased, or domesticated to a degree that ensures it will never return. In Houston, schizophrenia rules. By proximity, or *synomorphy* (similarity of form), the rider of the plane drifts along (in contradistinction to the pedestrian, the ruling subject of the old city) as morphing extension of the machines, forming with technology a shifting and uneasy coalition. Yet the drifters coalesce with the biota and trees, particularly when (even for the briefest of moments) they walk the plane. The trajectories along which riders move follow at least two speeds, both ballistic in nature. Along the first, bullet cars with cooled interiors push through the thick, humid phlegm. Along the second, even more viscous one, that of fear—*urban fear* (driving one to the false safety of closets, behind the barricades in one's enclaves)— another kind of bullet propels the action, but it is now aimed at the rider. It is no wonder that the commanding machine of this plane is the Chevy Suburban, all but achieving the dimensions of a suburban house and providing a protective, mobile, exoskeletal enclave (almost safe) along that tortuous trajectory of fear.

Fields

The commingling of machines and nature, be they houses, cars, or skyscrapers, set on a plain, or this crudely gardened version thereof, results in a Houston that is neither fully city nor tree (*pace* Christopher Alexander). Yet all the things that constitute the specific territory are more or less organically related, so that we can assume that it is, if not strictly or classically a city, then an ecology—or more theatrically, a flat planet—suggesting the powerful web of organic relations that makes Houston a palpable, cohesive reality.[10] Here variously gendered machines rather than pedestrians are the predominating species, and clean, cool air (rather than the atmosphere of Paris or the *energy* of New York) is the determinant commodity. The plane, with its zoohemic canopy of trees, forms a carpetlike subecology[11] dominated by dappled light, the collective purring of a panoply of machines, the invincible stings of mosquitoes. The planetary impression becomes even more compelling as the reader ascends. Suspended overhead in a skyscraper, two distinct strata or fields are apprehensible, one sandwiched atop the other: the zoohemic field below, the air space—the aerial field—above.

This huge bag of air is articulated by airplanes, helicopters, and the grandiose machinations of weather, which roll into the upper strata either quietly or with terrifying fanfare. Shaped like the whacked-out species of an exotic aquarium—huge partially disintegrated flounders, schools of drunken piranhas, bloated whales— slow, fast, frazzled, mostly opaque, and surrounded by wisps of indecisive grayish-brown mists, clouds often operate in opposite directions. Distemper: entire seasons pass in minutes, raising or dropping the temperature, making the surprised and totally innocent drifters under the canopy change their clothes as if models working the runway. Or thunder poised to deliver. Flashes that, like a giant Pert chart, draw the most random connections, cloud to cloud, cloud to building, cloud to ground, independent along the horizon, hideous verticals etching cracks in the black heavens destined for human disaster. Or rain, totally ignoring gravity by operating in any conceivable direction, up, down, sideways, toward you, and away from you sucking you into its destiny. Nature rampant. Unlike the lower strata, this huge stadium seems underdeveloped—begging for more towers, more air traffic, more lights, introduced, if for nothing else, to counteract the forces of nature, to challenge its total dominance. As it stands now, nature shares the ground with artifice, while the bag of air rules above, if it weren't for pollution.

Brown fumes. Fiery sunsets. Pollution fills the days when the weather rests. The totally still, yellow girdle of haze binds the sky and the ground together. Creating a third ecology, the vapor drops invisibly through the canopy of trees to slip into the drifter's nostrils, lungs, and eyes: sinus capital of the world. Yet it is only above the canopy, with the benefit of foreshortening, that pollution builds its body and makes its demanding presence visible. Like some immense unwanted backlash, the pollution-as-surplus reminds us of the price of our total mobility.

Two ecologies, two modalities (speeds) of circulation and appearance. The two strata touch, as do the two speeds, when the freeway hews its way through the green carpet to merge with the air space. In these gashes the two worlds are sutured together, or more precisely, the motorway adjoins the air space by delaminating from the plane. Submerged in the lowest stratum of a major freeway intersection, literally driving (at warp speed) on the underside of the ground ecology of the city, the rider is brought to a realization. In fact, all brushes with the outer margins of the various ecologies of the city, whether here at the base of the hierarchy or at its very top, hovering in an air vehicle while rapidly traversing both ecologies, tend to throw the whole into focus. Such realizations, frog's-eye or soaring eagle perspectives, are shapeful and at least partially extraspatial. They bring out of the scattered suggestions of wholes or megashapes that the rider senses while operating on freeways, or when arriving at large openings in the ground plane such as an airfield, a sensation of traveling along the tangent of the ecological envelope. While this may appear more evident in an airplane, it is more sensational when you dip underneath the ground ecology (as in the great freeway cloverleaf), possibly because the vehicle operates along a curve whose origin is somewhere above drivers, swinging them out of, yet against and into, the crust of the earth that serves as the carpet's ground.

Sprawl

Flying in over Houston from the east, a late winter afternoon, with the western light rushing in parallel to the ground creating endless shadows (and the Gulf vs. Canada weather war cooperating by staying away), one sees the holey plane emerge in all its tattered, uncouth ungainliness. Simultaneously, the very material that defines the holes comes into focus, known as sprawl. In sprawl, units, swatches, zones, and domains come to the fore, and since the zoohemic canopy is now its lowest photosynthetic self, the observer can read through the trees for the hundreds of thousands of houses, the meandering streets, the cul-de-sacs, the arteries, and the sinuous freeways. Sprawl is the very motor of this entire plane. Sprawl's erratic leapfrogging across the protean field is the driving energy.[12] Combine weak controls, a huge domestic economy, and the will to live "away from the city," and you have sprawl: *Go west, young man* (and all itinerant family members and paraphernalia).

■

One of the dominant megashapes in the suburban metropolis is so close to home that it is hard to see: the vast agglomerations of identical single-family houses on various-sized and -shaped lots. At first we may hesitate to refer to them as shapes, since it is only the interior reading that is distinct and clear while at the perimeter, at the locus of the figure, formlessness prevails. Furthermore, the tentative shapeliness is only readable from an eagle's perspective. In the final analysis, sprawl, just like the zoohemic canopy, is a megashape because of the prevalence and predictability of the internal equation: many houses and lots held loosely together with curving streets, often ending in cul-de-sacs and with one outlet to an artery.

The common view of sprawl is that it is chaotic, disorderly, ugly, and confusing— an additional example of the bias in favor of totalizing views of the environment. This doesn't negate the potential of increasing shapeliness, finding more effective uses or functions for the ungainly in-between at the perimeter of each unit of sprawl.

The internal nature of the sprawl unit is both rudimentary and crude, and in need of evolution. The orientation of the house is totally dependent on the platting, with no regard for the compass, the landscape, or prevailing ecology. Inefficient and wasteful, sprawl's true power and success lie in its economic and social effectiveness. Consequently it will take a lot of Jeffersonian (agrarian) persuasion to transform this Hamiltonian (mercantilist) success story. Put differently, sprawl is much like the Jeffersonian grid—Hamilton doing Jefferson—and the next evolutionary stage may be to tamper with this bias.

Oceanic Grammar

In the air or on the road, the clashes between the zoohemic and the aerial put the drifter in touch with what Baudrillard calls the "astral."[13] This may also be particularly European (East Coast too?), but the sensation one has when, for the first time, a tumbleweed crosses the highway somewhere on former Route 66 with no other car in sight makes one's ancestral home burst, releasing the rider within or from its (oppressive) security into the open, never to return. "How can anyone be European?"[14] The sensations referred to here cluster around the notion of speed, or better, *the notion of motion.* In Houston, it is not an exaggeration to suggest that the prosthetic is neither the car nor the air vehicle *but the drifter's legs.* Thus, coming from a pedestrian past, bursting onto the scene of the vehicular (and its associated velocities) clearly demarcates a takeoff that is *beside reality* as one once knew it. One lurches not just into a more rapid disappearance of what is seen in the rearview mirror, but also into the future (Virilio). Notwithstanding Baudrillard's point that "driving produces a kind of invisibility,"[15] the shape of the setting for those "pure objects" becomes more visible. This is more truly the case when the trip is repeated over and over again, a sensation Baudrillard clearly never experienced. The shape of the city's ecologies appears at its margins but, more important, during *repeated* trips along those margins. This exterior shapefulness is more conceptual than actual, held in place by mental constructions made of sporadically gathered shape fragments rather than physical continuities.

These external visions of shape are propped up, but now from the *inside,* by additional visions of shape, both more contiguous and more pervasive. To drive inside the zoohemic ecology—which includes trees, incessantly drawn at the periphery of one's vision—builds an additional understanding of shape that may not be exactly synomorphic with the external shape of the ecology. However, counting the particles of a field, rather than establishing the parameters of the field itself, touches on another grammar of shape—a grammar that is oceanic. However fractal and seismic the oceanic experience may be, it is also smooth and voluptuous. The continuous underside of the leafy canopy supported by countless tree trunks forms an inverted mountain chain of green that begins to build—once again through repetition—a conception of an inside. This inside is in no way trivial, particularly since it substitutes structurally for the loss of European city form. As city form, Houston interiority is very different from, say, Parisian interiority. Where the latter is constituted by the street, the verticality established by the perimeter block, and is propelled by pedestrian subjectivity, the low-slung green canopy establishes a pervasive almost-domestic intimacy that in the European city can only be had inside the residential block, in the warmth of a house. Thus Houston is at any one location a giant *room* as well as an ocean of endless surfaces. This inner field-and-room, produced through a trajectorial subjectivity, is held in place by two planes: the ground and the canopy of trees. Both planes undulate. The *fieldroom* is not a space in the European (Euclidean) sense but a constantly warping and pulsating fluidity.

The pedestrian, painstakingly circumscribing the blocks of the old city, harbors no doubt about what moves and what is fixed. In Houston, the speeding car projects itself into a space that is never formed, forever evolving, emerging ahead while disappearing behind. This creates a liquidity in which the dance and the dancer are fused in a swirling, self-engendering motion promoted by the darting of the driver's eyes, touching (because so intimate, so familiar) street, canopy, house, adjacent car, red light, side street, radio station Tejano 106.5, car upon car, instruments, tree trunks, joggers, barking dog, drifting leaves, large welt and dip, patch of sunlight. This is a navigational space, forever emerging, never exactly the same, liquid rather than solid, approximate rather than precise, visual but also visceral in that it is felt by the entire body, not just through the eyes and soles of the feet. The body in this liquid space is suspended, held and urged on by the trajectory.

The zoohemic and the aerial fields, invested by various velocities ranging from Suburbans to helicopters, pop out and disappear. On rare occasions nature draws the two strata clearly, and for a brief moment their innate fluidity is arrested. 7 A.M. DECEMBER 29: a weather front has drawn a blanket of clouds across the metropolis, so low that the tops of skyscrapers brush it. Not yet completed, the blanket gapes to the east, and the sun, like a child's flashlight, illuminates (not his momentary tent but) the airbag between the top of the zoohemic and the underside of the cloud cover. The light from the sun paints all the eastern facades of the skyscrapers—giant pilotis-candles supporting the sky. The huge window to my east burns bright red, while the sun rises up and out to create an eventual Arctic-scape of the cloud cover's upper surface. The sun has drawn a new section of the city.

The similarity in form between the two assemblies (tree trunk/canopy and skyscraper/cloud cover) posits the first determining structure or shapefulness of the two ecologies. Like stacked tables, one sits on top of the other. Then at closer scrutiny, the upper table pokes its skyscraper trunks down through the zoohemic canopy to the ground, thus originating in the lower ecology, literally growing out of it. The clear definition of the two fields, and the air space in particular with its momentary ceiling, forces the intimacy first established under the trees to include the entire metropolis. Air and biota are merged to form a doublespace, in which elements (tall buildings and certain vehicles) and fluids (air, sound, and smell) circulate freely.

Back on the ground, driving across the zoohemic field, the conceptual mingling of ecologies provokes additional cross-readings, but now horizontal: the freeway underpass, laminated away from the ground (that barren forest of concrete columns-and-canopy), takes on new value as the petrified token of the dominating ecologies of the metropolis, the concrete columns as so many artificial limbs mending the rift in the green hewn by the freeway itself.[16]

Entortung

J. B. Jackson's westward-moving house haunts Houston.[17] As one drives east-west along a street of modest houses, two remarkable rhythms occur. The street begins to roll like an ocean. Long shallow swells threaten to bounce riders from their seats while the houses, of which many are partially overgrown with vines, tilt ever so slightly, (further) revealing the tropic instability of the ground. The combination of the rolling street and the tilting houses is deeply unsettling. Everything moves (as in a sped-up geological flow). Every element is detachable, ready to go. The westward-moving house could have originated in some Heideggerian clearing in the Schwarzwald, but Jackson chose to begin the story on America's East Coast. At the beginning of its trajectory the house still had a basement. As it migrated farther west—and it sometimes did so because the settlers brought their houses with them—it was modified to respond to the next move. Among the first modifications was leaving the cellar behind, replaced by a set of rocks placed simply on the ground to serve as point supports. The final transformation of the frontier *Urhaus* is the contemporary mobile home, still the cheapest and fastest way to own a home, since it can be delivered like a car the following day on the basis of a loan amortized over a ten-year period. The tendency to make things lighter and more mobile goes hand in hand with what Karl Popper called the ephemeralization of technology, the suggestion that all technology will evolve from clocks to clouds. The tilting houses (they sit on the same type of supports as the westward-moving house, now made of mass-produced concrete blocks) are an expression of the *ephemeralization* and an *uprooting* of the house; severed from the ground, it shifts its status from build-ing to furniture—the house can now be part of the next move. The rolling street (a reminder of the clay gumbo out of which Houston arose) gives the experience of driving in this flat city the feeling of being held hostage on a subdued roller coaster. The rolling is not at all confined to the poorest parts of the city but characterizes the entire secondary street grid—and every house has, had, or will have a bad foun-dation day. Unsettling as it may seem, the rolling rhythm of the road and the racking of the houses (real or imagined) produce a strange echo of what in New York would constitute a city beat, though here it is not bebop but blues, zydeco, and cumbia. This rolling of the ground suggests that not only are the elements upon it unstable (and rhythmic) but the very field itself is the ultimate demonstration of metropolitan *Entortung* (uprootedness) which Georg Simmel began to map out in his essay "The Metropolis and Mental Life" and Massimo Cacciari used as one of the bases for his *Architecture and Nihilism: On the Philosophy of Modern Architecture.*[18]

In Houston, the entire foundation of the ground-level ecology is soft, rhythmic, and unstable, held together by the roots of the canopy of trees, creating the absurd impression of a city suspended from the treetops from which its cars, riders, and roads gently swing. At any rate, the ground is a detached ground, the house an in-finitely migrating detached house that follows in a slow attenuated progression the same Brownian trajectories as do its associated deputy paraphernalia—the car and the dweller, emblems of a restless urban matrix, continually on the move.

Stim and Dross

Space is granted little physical presence on the plane of this planet. Dominated by motion, time, and event, all components of this complex hide an essential vulnerability: trees die, cars and markets crash, and the air slowly kills. In fact, in Houston air functions much like our skin, an immense enveloping organ, to be constantly attended to, chilled, channeled, and cleaned. Pools of cooled air dot the plane, much like oases in deserts. Precariously pinned in place by machines and human events, these pools become points of stimulation—*stims*—on this otherwise rough but uninflected hide, populated only by the *dross*—the ignored, undervalued, unfortunate economic residues of the metropolitan machine. Space as value, as locus of events, as *genius loci*, is then reduced to interior space, a return to the cave. In these enclaves or stims, time is kept at bay, suspension is the rule, levitation the desire, whether of the office, the house, the restaurant, the museum, or the ever-marauding Suburban. Outside, the minimization of time is the dominant force that draws lines on this erratically littered surface and gathers its pools of energy. Once the time lines are seen to coincide and overlap, they begin to curl and twist. Our plot thickens at the Galleria—Houston's giant shopping spree, where the pistons and cranks of the metropolis have compressed more buying power into one single horizontal concatenation than in the entire region—and at the oil company office park euphemistically known as Downtown, where again the metropolitan muscle is flexed, but now vertically to sculpt the ultimate urban physique. The entire downtown as megashape is the token of all American downtowns. In a less obvious manner, time dominates still other forms of thickening in the ecology. Many of these bulges are less physical than virtual: "there, another Exxon station, another Target," subtle, ever-multiplying as market bytes whose recurrences follow the logic both of the cash flow and the catch basin. Outside, these stims, at once retinal and rhythmic, like mild electroshocks on the plane, join to become the extended skin of the rider.

The new space emerging from the impulses of this huge envelope is transient, fleeting, temporary, and biomorphic rather than concrete, manifested, or striated. Barely visible to the classical eye, these forms appear as expanding ripples in one's consciousness: swellings, bumps, and grinds coursing through the nervous system. Erratic, unpredictable, the time line for the spatial event jumps, twitches, hums, and wiggles like an erratic hose in a gardener's grip. Yet the flow encourages, the speed comforts, the ride heals. The chorus of the multitude of familiar stims forms a signifying beat, tapping gently on the rider's visual domain—the optic pouch—which replaces the cone of vision of a more mechanistic time. This pouch is always changing its size, sometimes confined, as when one throttles through a tunnel of trees, at other times expanded to amorphousness as it fills out an abandoned lot, a leftover plot of plain, or when, in a flash, the pouch explodes like a parachute to include a stretch of sky.

Urban threats prevail in this huge ecological envelope. Largely hiding out in the spaces between, the threats are kept away from the stims. (Stims must not be implicated or soiled by harsh realities.) Clandestine at first, yet ultimately as palpable as the humidity, the threats rush to the surface. Environmental ones, made apparent by the metropolis as a large unified ecology, an envelope with its own air, a sloppy organ whose precarious health is clearly in question. Here the fear of miasma is real—Houston is one of the most polluted cities in the nation. And that of urban fear—the insidious force that atomizes the city like a scatter bomb into myriad cells each surrounded and enclosed by various forms of callused protective tissue (physical prowess, power in numbers, rent-a-cops, walls, gates, distance, electronics, guard dogs, lot size, borders, railroad or freeway barriers)—an entire physics of enclavism. We are talking warfare here. This strife propels and animates the ecology, much more than Ecology itself, maybe as much as the market force. Like myriad invisible nanomachines clandestinely at work undermining metropolitan sanity, fear has delaminated the stim from the plane, *Entortung* efficiently at work. In gaggles, stims agglutinate, skip, and leapfrog once the barometer of fear passes the critical mark. Yet among the middle class, the fear remains unspoken, silenced, merely illustrated in passing by the antiseptic crime statistics of the news media. In the street it speaks loud and clear. In fear's wake, in addition to the *great suburban escape,* come deed restrictions, restricted numbers of sewer hookups, zoning, alarms, and armaments: a few hundred thousand registered guns. Guns and gas—the propellants of the metropolis on the run. To what end is all this paraphernalia, when according to recent polls Houston ranks as the fourth most livable city in the United States? The answer surely leads us to the stims themselves, to their internal strength and, alas, to their vulnerability.

Stimulators

A colleague invites us to a reception given by an art patron. We traverse the plane and navigate the dross: a mental map, an address, a curving road, large lots and gigantic houses, the *de rigueur* smiling rent-a-cop. Our destination is a marvel of a house, a fantasy sustained by spectacular architectural scenography, various addenda (arresting decoration, whimsical furniture, subdued music), and the glamour of the party itself. The collusion is in fact a perfect one, between architects (the curved interior street), decorators (the towels arranged on the floor in the bathroom), caterers (the glutinous loot of shrimp), the art patron (her son's taxidermic hunting trophies), and her own overflowing enthusiasm. Suspended, the audience hovers in the fantasy. The house is a miniaturized Siena (turning abruptly, I search for a glimpse of the Palio) though not Siena at all, a marvelous polyphonic concoction that threatens all analogy in favor of the authenticity of the bristling stim itself. Here critique and skepticism fade in favor of the materiality of this specific event. It is an audacious one, surely costly, and marvelously intoxicating. Yet how does it hold up, or rather how is it held in place? Where are the invisible wires, the conceits of this theater of events? How and where does the dross come into play? After all, this fragment of Siena is held in place not by a city, by streets, piazzas, walls, or a city-state and its culture. Dislocated, the stim is suspended in the ocean of the city, but also suspended in time and out of context (Tuscany is far away).[19] When toggled on, the stim's shimmering lights attract its participants like moths sucked out of the darkness of the city. However, the smiling guard suggests that the suspense is not only momentary but precarious. And when the lights are turned low, the guests and caterers depart, the stim is turned off and the house and its occupants are again mere dross on the littered city floor. Indeed, light and darkness are inextricably bound. Like a cyberspace, the stim is anchored in place by technology and machines of every type, mechanical, electronic, and biological.[20] The *imbroglio* is vast, ranging from the Mexican laborers who tend the gardens to the architects' studies at the academy in Rome—it gathers, in a single sweep, lawnmowers and airplanes, but also sewage pipes, floral designers, pool installers, electrical power grids, telephone calls, asphalt, automobiles, the birds drawn to birdfeeder hubs, deathly silent air conditioners, mortgage banks, hunting rifles, and the little pink shrimps from the Gulf of Mexico. These interlocking systems have, in architectural practice, been taken for granted and ignored, or dealt with as a kit of parts, each component neatly defined and rendered independent. This array forms a complex *body* that must, in the wet of the postwar city, be seen for what it is, a partially self-steering, partially spontaneous, yet cybernetic agglutination of forces, pulsations, events, rhythms, and machines. The neglect of any of its interlocked systems may, despite a multitude of checks, locks, gates, and balances, threaten its existence. The Age of Integration has come to call.

stimdross

The metropolis, like the surface of a lake during a rainstorm pocked by thousands of concentric ripples, is bombarded by a million stims that flicker on and off during the city's rhythmic cycles. These stims steam and stir, oscillate and goad, yet each specific *Stimme* (voice) reverberates throughout the metropolis in a most selective manner: the art party draws a very narrow audience just as do the zydeco dance halls in Houston's Fifth Ward. Both are essential and vital elements of the full-fledged metropolis. The *Stimmung* (ambience) projected by each stim is fully understood and fully had by insiders only. Although as a *stimulus* the zydeco dance occasionally draws a group of (slumming?) upper-middle-class guests (and they are graciously tolerated), they remain aliens, however moved they may be by the dance and its inert *stimulantia.* And there is Hugo's Garage, a stim that lasts for an hour or two on Friday afternoons when his clients come to pay their respects. He is the much beloved and respected mechanic (he works on imports) whose diverse clientele come to stim: beer and cars; car-as-transport parked and briefly elevated to car-as-art, setting aside all class and money distinctions between the aficionados. Simultaneously, a block away the hoods on a dozen cars go up (and the tiny lights turn on) to wire the iron-clad Hispanic Parking Lot Stim. Men gather around, the echo of a cumbia projected from several car radios envelops the momentary brotherhood. Open treasure chests, the stationary cars project back in time and place (to common culture and history)—*Bulevar de Sueños*, a telling balance to the *carro*'s otherwise futuristic prowess. A tiny sampler from the menu of "a million stims."

Ranging from the Family Dinner to the Card Game, all stims are held precariously in place, intensity, and motion by the metropolitan physics of "walls, particles, and fields." Metropolitan life is concentrated in these stims, and we live as if our life depended on them.[21] The common tendency to focus all attention on the stim ignores the fact that it is a living organism, machines, a behavior setting, in short a manifold shale of wonderful complexity. As such it is dependent on its talons and its backwoods (its lacunas), first the ocean of the metropolis, then the world. The inadequacy of the binary opposition of stim and dross is becoming evident (the legacy of our stale language and its profound grammatical limitations). Only in the hybrid field of *stimdross* may we begin to rethink and recover from this *holey plane* some of the many potential futures.

■

Driving along Highway 59, one of the central freeways in Houston, going west (or south), the roadway suddenly drops below grade, and the neighboring streets bridge over while drivers race down a concrete canyon, crossed by overpasses for some four or five blocks. This is the result of neighborhood action. A group of well-to-do citizens convinced the city to sink the freeway to lower the noise (and maybe put an open trench between them and their less affluent neighbors).

Driving the freeway you may see a lone observer. Just as you begin the descent into the canyon the observer looks right at you, then down at you, until he disappears above you. Invariably they are alone, often leaning on the balustrade, not moving. Or they walk back and forth, agitated, gesturing, and since their mouths seem to open and close—their heads are turning fast, back and forth, up and down—they may be screaming, or haranguing you. You cannot hear. They are the overpass people. Where they come from, who they are, no one seems to know. At first, you may think they are people from the neighborhood, looking down at you with a certain smug satisfaction. But in this town the well-to-do are not idle. So they come from somewhere else. Who is to know? They are clearly too few for a sample, or a sociologist. They range from the quiet kibbitzer to the enraged, suggesting that they are here for the action, for the movement, not the attention. Some may be students of motion, others radicals protesting our daily commute, or aficionados of the noise and smell of motor cars, or transcendentalists in search of a continuous external and loud mantra, an artificial river.

For us, the drivers of the superhighway, they are the others. Those who have time to spare. Those who don't have to (bikes are often held or parked next to the observer). Those who don't. Those who refuse. Not the leisure class, not the va-grants, maybe the mad, but mostly those who fall in between, those who refuse to be counted. We need them to remind us that all is not speed and progress.

Sparta's Revenge

Mycenae certainly was a small place, and many of the towns of that period do not seem to us to-day to be particularly imposing; yet that is not good evidence for rejecting what the poets and what general tradition have to say about the size of the [Trojan] expedition.

Suppose, for example, that the city of Sparta was to be deserted, and nothing left but the temple and the ground-plan, distant ages would be unwilling to believe that the power of the Laconians was at all equal to their fame. Yet the Spartans occupy two-fifths of the Peloponnese itself but also numerous allies beyond its frontiers. Their city is not built continuously, and has no splendid temples or other edifices; it rather resembles a group of villages, like the ancient towns of Hellas, and therefore would make a poor show. If, on the other hand, the same thing would happen to Athens, one would conjecture from what met the eye that the city had been twice as powerful as in fact it is.

We have no right, therefore, to judge cities by their appearances rather than their actual power . . .

—Thucydides, *History of the Peloponnesian War*

The Other City

Two cities—or better, one city and its other—serve as poles in a speculation that permits us to race across the suburban metropolis. In this duality, ancient Athens and Sparta are seen to outline two divergent trajectories. Both have had considerable consequence for modern civilization. In the West, the eternal city—*stenstaden* (the city built of stone) as the cradle of civilized life in all its turbulences and lulls—is well established and may be emblematized by ancient Athens. The ultimate city-state, Athens gained its importance from high visibility: its built environments and its "words and deeds." Sparta, left as mere archaeological specks on the Peloponnesian fields, gained its place in history not because of monumental built markers, but because astute historians make us remember.

Athens, the site and stage for the birth of Western philosophy (Plato and Aristotle) and politics with its agora (plaza) and Acropolis, are etched deep on our cultural screen. In Hannah Arendt's *The Human Condition*, the ideal citizen—the *bios politikos*—whose heroics were displayed in "speech and action—in *lexis* and *praxis*" (rather than through force and violence)[22] remains the standard against which, with considerable loathing, we judge modern politics. In Athens freedom was found in the bright lights of the public realm, not in the darkness of the household sphere. It is deeply disturbing to a sensibility formed in the Athenian agora that the modern *bios politikos* appears both *disembodied* in the eerie light of the TV screen and in the very *center* of that ancient private darkness—the living room. As long as we remember Athens, the suspicion will remain that the unseen parts of the politician's body are on their own nefarious errand.

The ancient procession of the Panathenaia snaked diagonally across the agora in the third century B.C. and weaved and stumbled up the rough steps of the Acropolis to rest, momentarily, in the Propylaea to overlook the highly complex and unusual Erechtheion to the left, and to the right the most glamorous and sophisticated of all temples, the Parthenon. Here all the mysteries of architectural composition and human ritual, even the "architectural promenade," were brought into one miraculous assembly. But, as in all tragedies, there were villains too, just across the way in the Peloponnesos.

If Athens was the city of light, wisdom, and culture, Sparta was the dark city occupying the plains of Peloponnesos. In Thucydides's words, Sparta "had little to show for itself," and the little we know about the physical manifestations of the Spartans' undeniable power seems ephemeral—territorial as in distancing rather than physical as in the built. Thus, Spartans met under the *skias* (canopy) rather than in the *stoa* like the Athenians, and when the young Spartans fought to practice for war, there was no *gymnasium* but a *platanistas*, a field surrounded by a row of plane trees and a moat, into which the losers were thrown at the end of the bout. Sparta seemed to have had little invested in permanence but everything in territory and *action*, in warfare—the illustrated version of capitalism. The household sphere was equally modest, a mere group of villages spread, seemingly at random, on the plain. The similarities with the modern suburb are uncanny, and the evolution is undeniable; the Spartan phalanx of soldiers in formation has been exchanged for the high school band, or (for a more functional simile) a loose formation of real estate agents demonstrating von Hayek's concept of "spontaneous order" by comparative price setting—and the *platanistas* for the baseball diamond, but with the same laconic vocabulary of form and demarcation. Sparta as the original suburb has come back to haunt the city. This trajectory is not straight, since it has commingled with other parallel force fields that are peculiarly American, begun with the Puritans and continued by the founders and custodians of the republic.

Virgin Fields

Theoretically, time travel permitted, a daredevil flyer could land on the Lawn at Thomas Jefferson's University of Virginia. Not because the Lawn is as large as an airfield, but because its fourth side was missing (that is, until McKim, Mead and White closed it in 1895). While our hypothetical Jeffersonian aviator responds to his savage heart, the New Urbanists,[23] like McKim, Mead and White, attempt to close and dam all apertures in the Open City.[24] These diverging desires begin to hint at the complex struggle between nature and civilization, freedom and control, that still reigns in the modern metropolis.

Jefferson, president and architect, may have housed, "in speech and action," both the head of the frontier's people and the savage heart of their artists. His university at Charlottesville, begun in 1779, displays what one writer calls a "pervasive inconsistency" in dealing with the confrontation between civilization and nature.[25] Jefferson's inconsistency is dramatically built into the separated worlds of black and white in Monticello, yet at the university the same inconsistency may be the best one could do in face of the irreconcilable opposition between head and heart.

The missing closure of the three-sided U-shaped plan (and the itinerant outlying parallel I-shaped bars) had two explicit intentions: to remain open to expansion, and poetically to allow the full view of the Virginia wilderness. This breach of the perfect architectural composition allows us to see the Lawn as both piazza and pasture—as place and seat of community and as clearing in the wilderness, momentarily held back. Yet this double awareness undermines both, and installs a permanent oscillation between open and closed (Duchamp's door). The Jeffersonian inhabitant of this virginal, Virginian landscape was the "democratic husbandman" who stood (or shifted his weight from one foot to the other) between nature and civilization, thus constructing a *middle landscape*. As David Bell writes in his insightful essay of 1983: "Jefferson invented a 'middle landscape' for America. The middle landscape is neither wild nor refined, it is the *mise en scène* for the necessary condition of 18th century man."[26] On the verge of the twenty-first century, it may very well be that this middle zone is a most important inheritance that, variously and radically transformed, is our last frontier. Jefferson's "garden republic tilled by the husbandman" has changed its custodian but the gardening must go on, not because our rationality is at stake but because our savage heart is.

The quad that Jefferson laid on that "virgin" field, because of its nearness to nature and future (expansion), was brittle, or better jointed and elastic, bending in the wind to accommodate but also dismembering itself to meet nature and to face opportunity. Thus laid down, *weakness* of form permeates the university buildings too. But it is a complex weakness. The ten teaching pavilions, all distinctly but subtly different, are held in place by the continuous portico. Yet the pavilions' diverging characteristics reveal ten agendas that, although held by the (almost) rigid arcade, challenge the singularity of the entire composition. Hovering between order and individuality, the University of Virginia begins to reveal its complex dual identity.

At first the portico appears perfectly rigid, as seen in a drawing of 1824, but as built it steps in segments down the slope of the landscape, making sectional breaks, some quite awkward. A certain weakness gives in to the real contours of the landscape rather than staying the course of an ideal plan. The reason may have been to save money by minimizing excavation or costly reshaping of the land, or, by mimicking the land, to reflect a certain reverence for or conspiracy with the natural—the pragmatic and the poetic.

Further complexities are revealed in "the successive lengthening of distance between the pavilions," which produces forced perspectives that make the mountains appear closer when seen from the Rotunda, while from the open side of the quad the Rotunda appears farther away—again *work on the distance,* revealing the desire to have urban monumentality while remaining close to nature.

Individualized, each pavilion speaks of a freedom desired, however disguised as "variety . . . to serve the architectural lecturer,"[27] but each is restrained by the portico. Yet this encounter between pavilion and portico is problematized by sometimes having the columns of a pavilion literally step over the portico, while at other times they stand behind. This complex intertwining, combined with different architectural expressions (all within the productive confines of classical *taxis*),[28] reveals that the quad is approximate rather than precise, weak rather than rigid, open rather than closed.

Organic, quasi-metabolic, the university as Humpty-Dumpty, with arteries as porticos reluctantly holding the pumped-up pavilions, spills, behind curving walls backed up by rows of student hostels, into gardens. Here an uneasy and incomplete or unfulfilled communion between husbandmen and nature is played out. Uneasy, since Jefferson believed that we would never comprehend the *modus operandi* of nature.[29] Incomplete: enclosed and domesticated in kitchen gardens, nature slipped surreptitiously inside civilization, but at the same time, at the missing fourth side of the quad, it held back so that wilderness would be at a proper distance. Oscillating, doubtful, or more positively pragmatic, multifaceted, and prepared for the "just in case," the university and nature are profoundly intertwined. David Bell writes of it as "a stochastic unity composed of a hierarchy of diversities which accepts the occurrence of chance events and change within an ordered framework."[30]

American railroads, according to the geographer James Vance,[31] were built to climb hills faster and turn curves sharper than English railroads, to save time and money. The same pragmatism is displayed in Jefferson's opening to future development (an attitude that McKim, Mead and White did not share when they closed the Lawn, which in turn opened the door to the next generation of university builders, who ignored the quad in favor of more suburban models of development). The poetic dimension of Jefferson's university—the appeal to the savage heart— enters the quad from a different direction than concerns for economy and efficiency. Back at the Puritan clearing, the wilderness was held back by the axe and the adze. Here on the Lawn, framed by the two assemblies of building and portico, wilderness is willed into place by the eyes of the subjects inscribed on the lawn— a shift from technology and brawn to *appreciation—at a certain distance*. Both subjectivities presumably knew that once the axe was laid to rest and the eyes lowered, the wilderness would rush back to reclaim.

Two decades before Thomas Jefferson became president, the Continental Congress established through the instruments of the Land Ordinance of 1785 and the Northwest Ordinance of 1787 what became known as the Jeffersonian grid, though it was a compromise between the agrarian ideals of Jefferson and the mercantile drive of his adversary Alexander Hamilton. Jefferson's vision was of a "valueless" public domain, tilled by husbandmen sent, as it were, on a Virgilian errand.

Here the grid had both *heart and head*, but harsh economic realities (Revolutionary War debts) and pressures from urban mercantilists added an economic twist that turned the grid from the public realm into an essentially private domain. The country was divided into commodity before it was fully explored. (A procedure, incidentally, contrary to the Law of the Indies of some two hundred years earlier, which was the final result of years of practical experience—there the law as theory was the mere confirmation of a process that had already taken place.) The "contents" of the Jeffersonian grid, as agreed to by agrarian and mercantile interests, were just that: attached, leaving the grid to its own peculiar structural yet contradictory characteristics of simultaneous enclosure and openness, making statements such as Grady Clay's half-right: "And once Nature—whether recast in the form of real estate, water, lumber, grain or cattle—was priced and placed in markets, it was no longer Nature."[32]

In this way, western prairie was converted into urban commodity. The stretching of jurisdiction (power) and resources over immense distances left a widely dispersed built world, a dispersion that was made all the more obvious but also comprehensible by the ever-present six-mile grid. Power was not manifested in the built, but in the gridded land: monumentality, normally associated with built things, was transferred onto the immense territorial expanse and its associated geography. Through the abstract grid as cool instrument and rigid frame, wealth and power were surreptitiously shifted from property to sheer distance. However, the same grid had also turned the wilderness into nature, a nature that despite someone's ownership was still alive, and angry as in earthquakes, floods, and hurricanes, or benign as in Arizona and California winters.

Although Jefferson was quite a Parisian, the ethos of agrarian reach has affinities not with Paris, Rome, or Athens but with the obscured fields of Laconia and its principal city of Sparta. The similarity between the landowning Spartans and Jefferson's husbandmen is striking, particularly in light of the class division between the landowning ruling class and the second-class merchants on the Laconian field, and between the landowning farmers on the prairies and the eastern merchants. Paralleling the military concerns of the Spartans, we have similarly the western lands reserved for American army veterans and the makings of a suburban empire. In America's westward expansion, as in a military campaign, the geometer and the warranter had laid the groundwork and articulated the rationale for the radical mobility to come.

It is ironic that American academicians, so dependent on physical evidence, have left Sparta in the historical dustbin and concentrated their work on Athens—especially since their everyday lifeworld has become increasingly suburban, a radical shift from the architectural and philosophical splendors of Athens to the *laconic* minimalism of Sparta and its highly disciplined warriors, a shift from to *urbs* to *rus*. Thucydides noted that Sparta was a city of "discontinuity, lacking in monumentality" as well as "physical distinction." Suburbia, with its absence of monuments (leaving aside the shopping mall) and loosely connected enclaves, shares many of Sparta's characteristics. The similarities run deeper: Sparta may have compensated for its lack of physical distinction with an extremely tight-knit social system, replete with division of labor and class structure—physical distance is superheated by social proximity, our suburban ethos. The Spartans would approve of the joggers, even the golfers, of suburbia, since they were avid believers in fitness. Likewise they would not be surprised by the chain stores, since the wealth of the full citizens of Sparta was vested in landed property, while commerce was left to the lesser class, in this case to an invisible *franchise class*.

The trajectory constructed here ties the Spartan legacy to the American suburb. In the light occupation of land by the emphasis of land over buildings—nature over civilization—by class separation, by dispersal rather than concentration, and by order and discipline within despite the turmoil beyond, one assumes a deep-seated antipathy to the city.

■

The radical step from Jefferson's University of Virginia and its open U, via the Jeffersonian grid and its closed square, to the metropolis and its ever-changing metabolic formations provides the *panoramic view*. A core of explorations will provide the *middle distance*, while occasional others will establish the *atomic distance*, the scale of the user. This is the range of the architecture of distance. All of them produce their own distinct subjectivities.

A Certain Distance

This synchronic race across the architecture of American distance is meant to provide a calibrating device against which more immediate and current phenomena may be measured. American distance, to put it bluntly, is everywhere, whether it pertains to subjects or objects. Like genetic code, it underlies at least all spatial actions performed by Americans, including those that are psychological and interpersonal. This code has been socially constructed in complex interactions between dwellers, objects, and the continent. And it is still under construction.

Condensing everything we know about building and dwelling, there is always a "certain distance" in America. This distance between objects and subjects is the emblem of our ethos of dwelling. Distinctly separate from the European ethos (in which distances are fluctuating, ambiguous, or simply lacking), the American distance ranges from the first distance that the Puritans inserted between themselves and England on the one hand and nature on the other, via E. T. Hall's *Hidden Dimension*[33] to the commuter distance between downtown and suburb. Loaded, this ever-present distance is specific and certain. Yesterday it smelled of fresh-cut logs, while today it is perfumed with the latest deodorant but still within range and reach of a bullet.

How it began we can at best speculate about, and only metaphorically. Perry Miller wrote beautifully in his essay on the Puritans of 1956 that a society so "despatched upon an errand that is its own award would want no other awards: it could go forth to possess a land without ever becoming possessed by it."[34] Thus *a certain distancing* was necessary. The threatening wilderness was kept at arm's length. In fact, the threat was all-encompassing, forcing those on the errand to distance themselves not only from the wild ahead but from England, the Quakers, the Anabaptists, and those of lesser means and minds. "On its own business," the Great Migration of 1630 was inscribed in a rigid mental and actual stockade that would ensure its purity, its rationality—a concerted effort to adjust *by separation* to life on the frontier. However, this helps only to explain the distance. We have yet to find its specific nature harbored in the modifier "certain," a nature that is not simply one of rejection but of heart and soul, sentimentality, fear, ingenuity, and power.

"And Nature" (if a sleight of hand is permissible), writes Miller, "in America means wilderness."[35] Despite the constant battle between civilization and nature, Americans were profoundly affected by their involuntary association with wilderness, which gave them, and particularly artists, an "impulse to reject completely the gospel of civilization in order to guard with resolution the savagery of [the] heart."[36] Compelled to defend society's virtue, *distance* was kept to itself, to its own civilization, with all its associated temptations and sins. And what had begun as a utilitarian thrust to gain "wealth, comfort, amenities, power" became stunted, held up by a nagging sense that nature was not limitless; and once there was no longer a frontier, how would we sustain a savage heart? Through distance? Through each of us claiming a part of nature? And though stunted by the calculus of land speculation, is this still the certain distance between us?

Objects in this field, cloaked in a certain loathing, appear at first cut loose from their infrastructure. But the emptiness between becomes the very geology of human interaction. No wonder then, when ten persons board an empty bus, that they carefully disperse themselves by calculating the proper suburban distance. Like birds on E. T. Hall's telephone wire.

The nature of this distance is profound and complex. Urbanity, that mode of togetherness that dominates European city life, is also present and all-pervasive on the American scene, but very different in nature. European travelers in early America found to their surprise that even in the most distant and primitive hut, far from Boston, Philadelphia, and New York, the occupants were well informed through books, magazines, and mail. A *secondhand* urbanity (the metropolitan vapor) results. The street is exchanged for other channels of communication. By injecting information into distance, physical distance is overcome while still separating.

The specificity of the American dimension has its own *push and pull*, with evasive as well as revealing features. The young female college student lap-dancing for the out-of-town businessman can, thanks to the push of distance, remain almost virtual, hiding both her personality and sexual proclivities. With downcast or distancing gaze, the same woman walking home at night after a performance constructs a vulnerable distance that allow males to scrutinize intimately and undisturbed, a simultaneous push and pull.

In the suburban house, the intercom (prefiguring the Internet) becomes a way to tell the truth in the dysfunctional family by keeping out of arm's reach. Here frankness and emotion are held in check by distance. The same distance, when built into the size of lots, not only keeps houses apart but keeps economic groups apart through high land costs. The building of the Galleria in Houston did not just sepa-

rate shopping from the office space of downtown, therefore making the latter a mis-
nomer, but played out the loathing of the city and its evils deeply embedded in the
American distance. The American city may always have been on the run from itself,
first within itself, but now more dramatically away from itself. Houston is no different. As a dramatic manifestation of this urban self-loathing, Houston is on the run,
and, like most expanding metropolitan areas, is going west. It may in twenty-five
years join Austin ("a much nicer place") and leave "the undesirable" behind—as in
(imagined) ever-expanding lumpen proletariat. *Haustin* may in turn go south (for
even better weather and a beach), because too many of J. B. Jackson's westward-
moving houses have gathered in California. The polis on the move, like the inland
ice, leaves the moraine in its wake.

Yet the *pull* that compensates for this flight is always there, reining it in, substi-
tuting for the physical distance, humanizing it. Thus, frenzy about the Internet is not
just capitalism and technology at work and the final shift from hard to software, but
a profound manifestation of the nature of that certain distance. Odorless, the man-
icured lawns of suburbia have been exchanged for an electronic space in which
disembodied subjects frolic without obvious corporeal consequences.

The Protean Field

Georg Simmel, the German sociologist, began the important work that recognized
the return of the spirit of the invisible city and the subsequent metropolitan *uprootedness*, the enormous and radical socioeconomic change associated with the
emergence of metropolitan life. In the German word for uprootedness, *Entortung,*
the word *Ort*—place—reveals Simmel's recognition that place was absorbed and
carried along with the unstoppable flow of metropolitan speech. The *Ort* was also
the first utterance of the City, the first rubble forming clumsy walls that in turn
formed an inner space set against a violence beyond. Further elaborated, these
walls were rapidly turned into writing—for centuries the city was written in stone—
a fabric that, seemingly unchanging, supported the life of generation upon generation. However, the moment when the city slides away from being written to being
spoken is not only when the city disappears but also when the metropolis finally and
totally absorbs architecture. The absorption diverts architecture from being the primary building block of the city and forces it to fend for itself in the giant marketplace

of the metropolis. Some thirty years before the drift from stasis to mobility had reach its apex, Le Corbusier made at Algiers in his Plan Obus of 1930–1934 a valiant, or desperate, attempt to carry architecture beyond block-making. He attempted to refurbish an entire city in one single architectonic gesture, bonding transportation systems, commerce, and housing into one immense megastructure. Manfredo Tafuri wrote hauntingly in *Architecture and Utopia:*

> Absorb [the] multiplicity, reconcile the improbable through the certainty of the plan, offset organic and disorganic qualities by accentuating their interrelationship, demonstrate that the maximum level of programming of productivity coincides with the maximum level of the productivity of the spirit: these are the objectives delineated by Le Corbusier with a lucidity that has no comparison in progressive European culture.[37]

This may have been the last attempt to deploy architecture as a totalizing instrument, making a synthetic amalgam of built form and city culture using the entire anthropogeographic landscape. Within the Spartan trajectory there are potential bifurcations. Obus may have been one of them, where the traces of the phalanx, in the form of a freeway-city, get petrified—turned back on itself—and returned back at the gates of the city itself.

In the decades that followed Obus, the U.S. Federal Highway Act of 1956 separated the highway from its architectural counterparts (housing, commerce, and industry). Along separate trajectories, federal subsidies of housing (amounting to guaranteed mortgage loans that spawned a huge private housing industry) and the freeway program ended up in suburbia but forever apart. Architecture as the potential missing link in a major federal city-building program was unceremoniously left to the private sector. With the exclusion of state-sponsored architecture (in contrast to European democracies, the USSR, and China), *architecture became a consumer good*.

During decades as a commodity, competing with cars and Christmas vacations, architecture fared reasonably well, saved by its sheltering capacities and propelled by its appeal to the egos of the upper middle class and to the collective psyche of those who had even more, the captains of industry and the modern corporation. With its roots in the city severed, architecture, as a cultural enterprise, did not fare well. A couple of spectacular architectural projects (on hills or at ends of left-over vistas) set apart from the all-consuming metropolis make no city culture, but are mere sound bites in the news, or rest stops on the endless metropolitan journey. For Le Corbusier, the architect was the organizer, not a designer of objects. For the Spartans the highway department is the organizer, even if, as Dick Tracy said, "the one who owns the sewage owns the city." The authority of the plan became a pipe dream. The disappearance of urban form, a disappearance perfected in Sparta, shifted the public away from colluding with architecture to shape city life.

Does the reader sense a tinge of regret here? You shouldn't, because there is none. For a change, the colonial elite did not bamboozle the people of Algiers. However, it seems clear that the Spartans do not have the answer either. Félix Guattari may be closer when he talks about a state of affairs "unstable, precarious, transitory," the *protean field* more like a chemical formula than like "homogeneous axiomatics."[38] Corbu had many aspects right in the Obus, such as aligning human work with everyday life, but he sought this alignment through *form* rather than through *free association*. The assemblage of humans, their machines, and their connections to the floor of the metropolis is still the key to a better world, but at present the manner of these associations is too Spartan to reach all the metropolitans. The ability of the Spartan metropolis to create markets, to move goods and services and high-paid personnel is exemplary, but its ability to construct "life, desire, science, creation, liberty" on a massive scale is severely restricted to the chosen few. The old Sparta exchanged architecture for a war machine; the new Sparta is displacing the architecture of the city with a consumption machine, whose unintended externalities may be its only redeeming features. Spending thirty-four man-years a day commuting, as workers do in Houston, is not one of these features, while speed and mobility for all would be. In 1997 six hundred houses were built inside Houston's loop (up some two hundred houses since 1996)—occupied in part by the middle landscape—while two thousand houses were built outside, suggesting that some Houstonians are getting tired of the commute. Despite the rigid internal geometries, the energy and speed of the protean fields, and the tendency for modern Spartans to be on the move, we can expect the fields to transform accordingly.

Radical Mobility

Tracing the marching orders of the Spartan phalanx, mobility (rather than stasis) comes into focus. *Mobility* is one of the keys to the suburban machine. But suburban mobility moves in contradistinction to pedestrian (city) mobility. The former is radical in nature, characterized by modern filmic sequences and jarring jump cuts, and although its origin may be the horse and its rider, it is the automobile and its rider that come into focus.

> It is a gloomy winter morning in Stockholm. Artificial light from windows, light poles, and cars carve a narrow, inexact, labile tunnel. Drifts of snow-slush, mostly along the edges of traffic lanes and between street and sidewalk, define an otherwise glistening black surface that seamlessly meets an equally black surround. Dark shapes of people and vehicles move like robots along seemingly predetermined tracks. The glum anatomy of an everyday winter morning some 500 miles from the Arctic Circle, where the day is as dark as the night.
>
> The year is 1961; Sweden is just about to change from left-hand to right-hand traffic. I stand at a large window in an office overlooking a major street. Exactly at 8 A.M., all cars, buses, motorbikes, and bicycles come to a halt, only to slowly cross from one side to the other. Inscribing sigmoidal curves in the glistening black surface—moving forever from the left to the right, as if part of some vehicular ballet—all drivers abandon for an instant their individual destinations to join this vast national collusion. Simultaneously along the tunnel-like network of roads all across the country the citizenry has its mobility rearranged. Now, abruptly untangled, Swedish traffic joins, in a straight line, the European continent below.

Roughly at the same time as the shift-over in Stockholm, particularly along the nebula of postwar cities—Tokyo, Taipei, Los Angeles, Houston, Orlando, Atlanta, Randstadt Holland, and the Ruhrgebiet—another event went by unseen. In the blink of an eye the city shifted from being primarily stationary to becoming predominantly mobile. The moment when pedestrians psychologically became drivers; when software as in communication superseded hardware as in streets; when total accessibility overturned "location, location, location"; when the hegemony of the city was overturned by a suburban ethos.

At this event the city lost its bearings and no longer served as the geological substratum for what was becoming an immense protean field. This is neither trivial nor simple. The realization that speed dominates stasis, and that stasis has become mere pause and rest, completely undermines the age-old concepts of *permanence and identity* in favor of *transformation and event*. The city is being swept away by the metropolis. This action does not just replace one noun with another, but radically turns one state of affairs into *a state of perpetual motion*. As a collective action—a verb more than a noun—the metropolis destabilizes our concepts of time and place. With the dissolution of the city into the forever-emerging metropolis, our existence slides into permanent mobility.

Voids and Vapors

Americans' tendency to distance themselves from each other, fueled by loathing and an abundance of space—resulting in a certain distance—is only one side of a complex national story of distance. The other side, almost its opposite, is the undeniable fact that Americans have always had to overcome distance. This was dramatically apparent in the sixty years after the treaty of 1783 which ended the American War of Independence. The initial north-south coastal axis began its rotation toward the continental western axis: the Louisiana Purchase of 1803, the Florida treaty of 1819, the Texas annexation of 1845, the acquisition of the Oregon Country of 1846, the Mexican Cession of 1848. The immense feat of crossing and laying claim to this vast land area must have stretched everyone's imagination and capability. The historian and essayist Philip Guedalla wrote in his reflections on the western tendency:

> It tilted the whole country in a new direction and gave its territories a new depth. One day, perhaps, the lines of the United States would be redrawn. Their main direction was still north and south along the Atlantic slope. But if the westward tendency grew more pronounced, the old direction of the country might lose its meaning and the lines of the United States would run east and west across the continent.[39]

If going west was like stretching a fabric of claim all the way from the east, it is no wonder that parts were skipped, left acknowledged but unaccounted for, leaving an immense plane of clearings as well as voids, blips, and lacunas. Between the push to make distance and the pull to overcome it may lie the root of the characteristic disjointedness of all American conurbations.

Although connectedness is the spirit of the city, and will probably remain so, the American version has always harbored a tendency to explode, to atomize and to spread itself as far apart as possible. Today this may be exacerbated (or made more possible, if you like) by the media of virtuality. Connectedness need no longer be physical. Robert Smithson may have set the agenda of kenofilia, the love of emptiness, in opposition to topofilia, the love of place. In his succinct description of the radical difference between the built fabric of Manhattan and Passaic, New Jersey, he suggested that the latter might have replaced Rome as a world city. To others these holes may appear idiosyncratic or simply invisible, mere jump cuts in the ebb and flow of the city. However, when focused on, the voids of the holey plane are clearly systematic, essential, and, as it may prove, fortuitous components of the ubiquitous American real estate machine. Leapfrogged, the voids are elastic blobs that allow the developers to hang onto their profit margins. The size and shape of the blob may in fact be a complex reflection of the dynamics of land costs, market forces, building practices, and peculiarities of local conditions. These voids might be evidence of someone's deep pockets, the result of rising land costs and the availability of cheaper land just beyond. Or they may be the result of the autonomous evolution of the form, what Albert Pope has called the ladder (where the formerly continuous grid gets cut off to create enclaves of development). Either way, these voids—a form of unintentional land-banking—are restored to a new potential. Are they the last microcosmic frontier of the city?

The conventional argument suggests that all we need to do is to fill in the holes and complete the destiny of a contiguous city. Pope cautions that such knee-jerk reactions fail to understand the new city. Instead, he seems to say, this galaxy of voids needs to fulfill its own destiny as discontinuity.

The usefulness of the map of voids, now recognized across the entire globe in the wake of the *cordon urbain,* can come into focus. Parts of this reflection are written longhand on one of the ninety thousand islands that dot the Baltic Sea between Stockholm and Helsinki. The care afforded these islands—the lacunas of the sea—

and the ensuing union between nature and culture hold a lesson for the corresponding lacunas of the Holey Plane: the domain of the voids is best put in the hands of a custodian, for it may not survive on their own. The nature and future of these voids are currently unclear. Pope suggests that they should remain so, although the real estate machine "thinks" otherwise. Yet, like animals (to paraphrase Luc Ferry, the French philosopher), these lacunas are the backside of the metropolis—the other—whose very nature is ambiguous.[40] It is the custody of this ambiguity that is one of the sources of our humanity. More specifically American, these voids (be they the atomized lacunas of the inner loops of the metropolis or the larger ones in the outer reaches of the urb) could serve as a national reminder of the once great, exhilarating push west embedded in the national character.

Simultaneous with the national stretch for overcoming distance, other compensatory steps emerged. The spreading of news, combined with advertising, rumors, and gossip, has since become a national pastime that today, with the help of telephony, TV, and the Internet, may have annihilated the very idea of distance. The spreading of metropolitan airs takes many forms, and some of them operate under the auspices of architecture and building.

Marfa, Texas

Driving west across Texas, you traverse one-third of the continental United States, but you may not count the rivers you crossed (about ten if you drive along the 30th parallel) nor notice the subtle but steady rise of the land (from almost sea level to 6,000 feet), even if you notice the change in climate (from humid to dry) and vegetation (from moss-covered oaks to mesquite). Most certainly you are not noticing that the rivers after the Mississippi are increasingly tilting west. And when you climb the Guadalupe and Davis Mountains (the tail end of the Rocky Mountains) and stop to study the map (one that displays the topography), it is evident that the great geographer has struck an arc with its origin somewhere along the 90th meridian in the Gulf of Mexico. The legs of this arc form a great V between the Appalachians and the Rockies, with the rivers following suit in between. Now you know you are going west—even the land tilts so.

You will find Marfa, a tiny town, sitting in the high desert, in the last of three huge "fields" bounded by the major rivers that make up Texas. In the first (going east to west), bounded by the Sabine and the Brazos, lie Houston and Dallas. In the second field, bound by the Brazos (for the argument skipping the Colorado) and the Rio Grande, lie Austin and San Antonio—Edwards Plateau and the Hill Country—and in the third, bounded by the Pecos and the Rio Grande, lies Marfa. The artist Donald Judd moved here in the 1970s to establish a place for art that he saw as a radical alternative to the museum, if not to the city. Benefiting from the declining population of towns like Marfa, he was able to acquire numerous buildings and tracts of land. Here he installed permanently his own and his friends' works of art, his primary residence and place of work. Aside from being hauntingly beautiful, Judd's Marfa holds many lessons.[41]

The decision by an international artist to move back to the land, while at the same time importing the city in the form of its most flagrant artifacts, is a display of the global reach of the *cordon urbain*. Largely depopulated and leapfrogged by the great western push, Marfa, Alpine, and Fort Davis, all tiny towns, are rebounding. But now, they re-form in the hands of urbanites (dude ranchers, semiretired lawyers and artists), with their peculiar mixture of values embracing conservation (as in an even greater distance) as well as the urban stim (extensive guest houses). Thus, writing about his ranch Ayala de Chinati (overlooking the Rio Grande), Judd asserted: "I've never built anything on new land," while at the same time he would throw a yearly party with the entire New York art world in place.[42] Having displaced architecture as its synecdoche, metropolitan suburbanism is a juxtaposition of lacunas (dross) and frantic activity (stim). And though while driving across this spectacular desert you may only meet tumbleweeds, you are still inside the complex vapors of the metropolis. These vapors—a cacophony of virtualities: TV, talk radio, telephone, Internet, magazines, newspapers, books, music, movies, urban sensibilities (as distributed in behavior, in city ways)—have replaced the ancient paraphernalia of the city: architecture, sewage systems, streets, plazas, and monuments.

Judd's "urbanization" of Marfa is both subtle and radical. Subtle, because his interventions came mostly in the form of cleaning up, repairing, and reversing the value of the abandoned space by giving the emptiness a stoic elegance and purpose. Radical, because he altered the relationship between human occupation and the land. The decision not to build on virgin land would, if taken seriously, change the trajectory of the metropolis. Radical, because with a shrewd sleight of hand Judd altered the relationship between art and people.

In a text outlining the intentions of his Chinati Foundation, Judd explained how art and architecture had been separated from the dweller and how they "do not have to exist in isolation."[43] Against the "bigotry of culture,"[44] which suggests that art is added rather than part of everyday life, art in Judd's world is folded in and turned into an aspect of daily life. Thus, in a large shed housing work by the English sculptor John Chamberlain, guests can also sleep. "Almost all spaces, especially if they contain art, should be livable."[45]

The Artillery Sheds, the Chamberlain Building, the Arena, the Mansana de Chinati, and the U-shaped Barracks are for me truly visionary. The simple spaces, the visible affection for the vernacular (a building tradition that is almost autonomous in that its exists in parallel with daily life), the subtle corrections of the given, the insertion of art, and the attention to dwellers and wanderers construct a field of parallels that defies synthesis, each in its own distinctness and quality. Stepping gently, yet spreading his arms to claim space and distance, Judd created a microcosm in which the voids are no longer distinct spatial entities but are built into space itself. This is the legacy of minimalism, particularly as set in big space. Yet in this specific case, the result is curiously devoid of ideology. So "spacious," so larded with in-betweens, with micro-space, with certain distances, Judd's Marfa is seamlessly bridging the gap with the region's simple past. Each strand, past and present, is a project in itself: the milled aluminum boxes, the spartan spaces for living, the large sheds, the desert, the metal houses. Running in parallel seemingly oblivious to the next, each project is on its own errand. Yet as a series of adjacencies offered to the world, all are wide open, and the wanderer, like a seamstress or a tailor, is free to sew his or her own web of life.

Judd's realm, greatly affected by the sensibilities of his former partner the Roman architect Lauretta Vinciarelli, is post-Tafuri, far beyond the exasperated objects of the architects Judd loved to hate. The buildings he bought do not form a physical totality. Despite Judd's iron fist, when content is added (exhibitions, meetings, visitor's programs, art projects, artists-in-residence) they form a cultural tissue that flutters in the gentle winds sweeping down from the Rockies to meet the wet mists of the Gulf below.

Standing in the Artillery Shed overlooking one hundred versions of Judd's aluminum boxes and the metal sheds through the wide windows, the parallels come into focus. Parallels between his art, furniture, and architecture on the one hand; on the other, the parallel between Judd's displayed art and the metal buildings beyond, the town. Disparate yet similar, these correspondences stem from one sensibility, long in the making, like Thoreau: "simplicity, simplicity, simplicity." Reading across the parallels, egged on by the subtle similarities, we may see an enactment of Alberti's dictum now enhanced—the house is a small town, and the town is a large house, the art is a small town, and so is the furniture. The dictum may again ring true despite its original simplifications, because the additional and parallel reflections make other and more complex computations possible.

■

It may be Texas, but as a peculiar coincidence another tiny town, Archer City, close to Wichita Falls and not far from Fort Worth, has likewise been inundated by the vapors of the metropolis. But here it is not art but books, and not an artist but a writer and a bookseller who is behind the inundation. Larry McMurtry, the author of *Lonesome Dove,* is also a passionate book lover/seller. Like Judd, the writer took advantage of the soft real estate market to buy up several buildings in the small town with the intent to "house a million books": as if he wanted to anchor one end of the spectrum of which the Internet bookstore amazon.com holds up the other—the local versus the global. McMurtry's introduction of books, and lots of books, into the world that was often the setting of his own books may in the long run be a more successful integration of the little town, its remaining culture, and the urban than Judd's Marfa. Time will tell. From a metropolitan perspective, the forced integration of books and small-town culture is not only typical but also one of the great benefits (there is more to sample); not only beneficial but also necessary and crucial. In it lies the formula of the metropolis at its best—a kind of alphabet soup, in which order and rationality (zoning) are much less important than rampant and excessive heterogeneity, an important remnant of the city culture.

The omnipresent metropolitan vapors are evident all across the holey plane, far and beyond the urban precincts. Distance is still being overcome by increasing speed and coverage in transportation and communication.

Going west has still its place in the American psyche. But there are many other turbulences, jitters, and pulsations that make up the book of distance: the daily commute; migratory patters of seasonal workers; the back and forth of Oklahomans seeking their fortunes in California: the going, the failure, the return, and the renewed attempts; the great African-American exodus north; the Trail Riders descending yearly on the Houston Rodeo uncomfortably sharing right of way with thousands of commuters on the feeders of the superhighways (the hoofbeat of the prairies juxtaposed on its metropolitan counterpoint: the hum of neoprene); the drive-to-drink from dry to wet counties still shaping Saturday traffic patterns in Texas; or the electronic hikes along the bitways of the computational galaxy. Consequently, below the steady national western flow lies, on a molecular level, a cacophony of Brownian motions that obscure and contradict all simple theories of distance on the North American continent. Yet *going west* may be the equivalent of a Maxwell's demon unifying all disparate movements into one, suggesting, wherever we go, that in mind we always go west. The full story of distance in American culture—its motions, voids, and vapors—has yet to be written.

III
Architecture Reconsidered

The city's long shadow fades in the dappled light of the suburban metropolis. The ancient palette of urban forms—Street, Boulevard, Plaza, Perimeter Block, Monument—are passed over by Stim, Megaform, Single-family House, Dross, and Distance. These in turn beckon us to find new ways of shaping the metropolis, now drawn from its rethinking. However, the step from reading to action is long and not easily taken.

Tafuri suggested that the metropolis has absorbed architecture, and I agree. But what does this mean? Does it undermine the direction of the discipline as it was shaped by the city? Is there something in "communities without propinquity," and the way their buildings are mere receptacles of events, that pushes architecture so far into the background that it only needs to register as image on the visual screen? Yet if we still take architecture to mean considered building—building plus reflection, "buildings with shadows" (John Biln)—must not this concept of architecture be reconsidered beyond mere image making, and with it the architect—under the auspices of the suburban metropolis?

In anticipation of a new metropolis, a pattern emerges. A widely scattered pattern in which the single-family house, as a microcosm of the metropolis and as the primary site of a vast array of modern concerns, takes new form and importance. In its wake numerous nuclei of architectural preoccupations find their focus: the relations between subjects and objects, the demise of ideology and the potential for freedom, the roles of the architect, and the emergence of a new generation of design machines.

The End of the Architectural Promenade:
A Portfolio of Images

17 *Distraction*

Distraction versus Concentration

What is at stake in the metropolis's absorption of architecture is architecture itself. In the city, architecture's role and importance were taken for granted. It was the building block of the city. In the suburban empire architecture is facing its toughest test.

In the city, architecture's relation with its dwellers was unproblematic, in no need of inquiry. Monument or perimeter block, the fundamental point and outline of everyday life, architecture had a seat at the high table, and it still has in cities like Paris, where presidents bet their reputation on *le grand projet*. In the suburb architecture may have become mere commodity.

The task at hand is to rescue architecture, no more, no less. Although complex and deeply ambiguous, I shall begin at the junction between objects and subjects. At the place that Walter Benjamin has defined as the moment of either *distraction* or *concentration*, of absorption *of* architecture or *by* architecture. Simultaneously, I shall address what in the suburban metropolis is the perimeter block's corresponding building block, the single-family house, by making it the formal focus and the stage on which the struggle for architecture is played out, now on the microscopic scale. Within the horizon of the house, the view is panoramic, in defiance of architecture's purported autonomy.

18 *The absentminded examiners*
The Parade, Berlin, early 1900s. Photograph by Waldemar Titzenthaler,
turn of the century.

We are in Walter Benjamin's Berlin of the 1910s, standing on the sidewalk of a grand boulevard (it may be Unter den Linden) watching a parade. A group of men look intently at us as they march by. Though they are civilians, they appear to be military men just out of their uniforms. Most probably, they are the fathers of the new Germany that will be known as the Third Reich. Shoulder to shoulder, united and strong, they march with purpose into their future—our all-too-painful past. Their gazes brush past our faces without focus. What is important is the gaze itself: the beam that bridges the depths of their eyes and our blank faces. It is hope, direction, and determination coupled with a certain absentmindedness, even self-indulgence, because the gaze doesn't see—it doesn't need to see since it has already seen what it needs to see: the marcher's version of the future. Through the benefit of hindsight we know that from our point of view the errand of these men was foolish, even murderous, since thirty years later they indirectly caused Walter Benjamin to take his life at Port-Bou. Yet he warned of these "absentminded examiners," in his classic "The Work of Art in the Age of Mechanical Reproduction":

> The mass is a matrix from which all traditional behavior toward works of art issues today in a new form. Quantity has been transmuted into quality. The greatly increased mass of participants has produced a change in the mode of participation. . . . Distraction and concentration form polar opposites which may be stated as follows: A man who concentrates before a work of art is absorbed by it. He enters into this work the way legend tells of the Chinese painter when he viewed his finished painting. In contrast, the distracted mass absorbs the work of art. This is most obvious with regard to buildings. Architecture has always represented the prototype of a work of art the reception of which is consummated by a collectivity in a state of distraction. The laws of its reception are most instructive. Buildings have been man's companions since primeval times. Many art forms have developed and perished. . . . But the human need for shelter is lasting. Architecture has never been idle. Its history is more ancient than that of any other art, and its claim to being a living force has significance in every attempt to comprehend the relationship of the masses to art. Buildings are appropriated in a twofold manner: by use and by perception—or rather, by touch and

sight. Such appropriation cannot be understood in terms of the attentive concentration of a tourist before a famous building. On the tactile side there is no counterpart to contemplation on the optical side. Tactile appropriation is accomplished not so much by attention as by habit. As regards architecture, habit determines to a large extent even optical reception. The latter, too, occurs much less through rapt attention than by noticing the object in incidental fashion. . . . The public is an examiner, but an absent-minded one.[1]

Back on the boulevard, in the spectacle of the city, the men march as the actors and we watch as the audience. As rapt bystanders we are part of the architecture, the backdrop for the events of history, only stepping stones in a narrative that is eagerly trying to get to the end, to a future that the marchers thought would be better than their present.

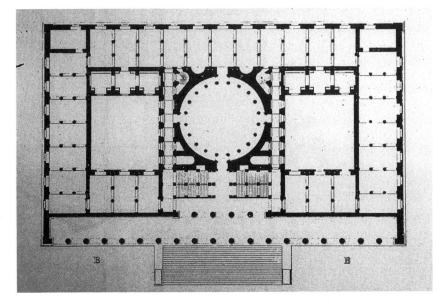

19 *Their plan*
Ground plan of the Altes Museum, Berlin, by Karl Friedrich Schinkel.

The metaphoric footprint of this narrative can be seen in the plan of a building not far from the boulevard: Karl Friedrich Schinkel's Altes Museum of 1823–1830, with its unbroken row of Ionic columns, Pantheon-like rotunda, and relentless matrix of exhibition rooms.[2] Here room upon room marches in an endless enfilade, mirroring the scene on the boulevard—the immobile bystanders are the walls, the space they enclose becomes the marching men, and the door leading from one room to the other, the inscription of one of the men in his city suit, top hat, and white beard. A mere pawn, his traces in the museum plan are minimal because fully descriptive of a disciplined marcher, driven by powers beyond him. The epitome of Benjamin's distracted subject is constructed in the *marche* of the classical Beaux-Arts plan. It is in apparent and vigorous opposition to this absentminded examiner that Le Corbusier's New Man appears, fully modernized, at the bottom of the ramp in Le Corbusier's Villa Savoye—the beginning of *le promenade architecturale*.

20 *The boxer*
Le jardin suspendu, Le Corbusier, 1928-1929. Immeuble Wanner, Geneva.

Full-fledged Corbusian man comes into view in Project Wanner of 1928–1929. In the application of the concept of the Immeubles-Villas of 1923 and 1925, he is shown in a drawing of an interior dressed in trunks and tank top pounding a punching bag in one of *les jardins suspendus.* A woman stands watching on a balcony (as a mother would watch a child). It could be his wife, or *la bonne*—her hands are resting on a railing on which a blanket hangs—as much a symbol for her as the punching bag is for him. The drawing shows the distinctive double-height space that became the insignia of Corbusian space of this vintage despite the constraints of what Colin Rowe has called the "paralyzed section" of the floors as tables, one on top of the other, that first appeared in the Dom-ino system of 1914. Aside from the open book on the table and the immobile female bystander, the suspended garden is vibrant with *le mouvement architecturale*: the oblong column, the curving wall, and a rope suspended from the ceiling taken directly from a jungle gym, the first trace of the architectural promenade and its technologies. In Le Corbusier's transformation, the marching man in the demonstration on Unter den Linden has become the consummate modern athlete, whose politics have receded in favor of the care of the body. "Culture of the body," says Le Corbusier, "is to care with wisdom for one's bodily frame—the human body, the most perfect machine in the world, the physical prop of our whole existence. The body can thrive or wither, be resplendent or decay in sickness or deformity. For this, adequate sites and environments must be chosen. It is for architecture and urbanism to create the means."[3]

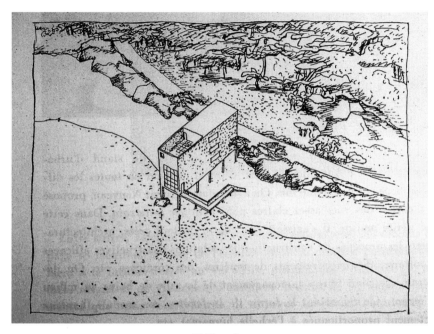

21 *His section*
Ramp and solarium: A Villa Next to the Sea, Le Corbusier, 1928.

Corbusian man arrives by automobile at Villa Savoye. Le Corbusier describes the arrival: "The auto enters under the pilotis, turns around the common services, arrives at the center, at the door of entry, enters the garage or continues on its way for the return journey: this is the fundamental idea."[4] He marches no longer in the company of others. The footprint is no longer the enfilade of rooms or the plan, but the entire array of roads and its extensions—the ramp and its associated technologies. The house itself is a mere stop on a much longer journey than the "circular ruin" the Altes Museum implied—"this is the fundamental idea." Le Corbusier continues: "The house poses in the middle of the open as an object, without displacing anything."[5] Once inside the vestibule, our man steps out of his city clothes and dons shorts and a tank top. Half running, his fingertips run absentmindedly along the handrail of the ramp that takes him to the floor of the house proper. "But we'll continue the promenade. After the garden on this floor, we climb via the ramp to the roof of the house where the solarium is."[6] The domain is no longer the plan but the section, and here at its cusp we have reached the end of the promenade. But Le Corbusier has more to tell:

> Arab architecture gives us a precious piece of information. It is appreciated while walking, with the feet: it is walking, while moving, that one sees the development of the architectural order. It is a principle contrary to the one used by baroque architecture that is conceived on paper from a fixed theoretical point. I prefer the insights of Arabic architecture. This particular house acts as a real architectural promenade, offering constantly varying aspects, unexpected and occasionally astonishing.[7]

Succinctly, elegantly, Le Corbusier offers us the entire agenda of a filmic or scenographic view of architecture, Benjamin's no-longer-distracted examiner absorbed by "the work of art." According to Le Corbusier, the new man is all attention and completely aware of "un schéma de poteaux et de poutres" (a matrix of columns and beams) as well as the site, the suspended garden, and the free plan. A superman who can do two things at the same time: pursue his everyday narrative while simultaneously appreciating architecture. By sleight of hand, Corbu attempts to bridge the gap between distraction and absorption, by fusing use, touch, and vision. But this is the architect's homunculus. On his own errand, the actual boxer, mundanely, sees the architecture only from the corner of his eye, while everyday life dominates his vision. Architecture's attention is held hostage by the demands of the day.

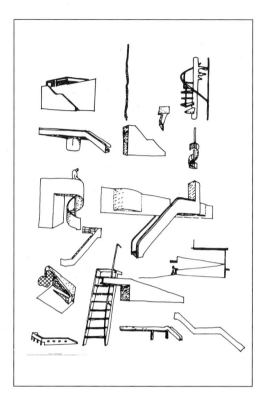

22 *The moving subject*
Sectional technologies, after Le Corbusier.

The enfilade of rooms in the Altes Museum marches endlessly in its own footsteps, one story laid on top of another. The doors as erect rectangles hint at the physiognomy of the pedestrian. This circularity must have appeared completely ridiculous to Le Corbusier, who saw the great errand into the modern world as a stair, corridor, rope, and ramp reaching up and away from the constraints of the past. The *Oeuvre complète* of the period between 1910 and 1940 was replete with sectional technologies, all promising speed, efficiency, and fortunes beyond.[8] This message was all too optimistic and thereby cast a critical light on the invisible seam between architecture and utopia, on architecture's ability to change life, to lead, and to fulfill life's promises.

23 *The end*
Plan Obus, Algiers, Le Corbusier, 1930.

The "pure topological field" recognized by Manfredo Tafuri in his interpretation of Le Corbusier's Plan Obus for Algiers was created by the serpentine strip-city that he wanted to overlay on the city and its environs. The entire region is turned into a *plan libre,* and the highway-city becomes the ultimate architectural promenade. It no longer merely suggests the optimal path through the "field" but is the central path, by containing within it a continuous presence of an entire population of "boxers." The architecture is absolutely synomorphic (similar or coincidental in form) with behavior. The promenade as a pedantic and didactic instrument for a privileged view of architecture has at Algiers become the only way to see. Furthermore, the locus of hope—*le jardin suspendu*—at the end of the promenade has rather anticlimactically become the on and off ramps to the linear city.[9] Clearly neither the only nor the last totalizing attempt by a modern architect, the Plan Obus is symbolic. A major setback for the belief in architecture's total instrumentality, coupled with the end of the architectural promenade as administered by the architect. Determinism, mastery, and heroics laid to momentary rest.

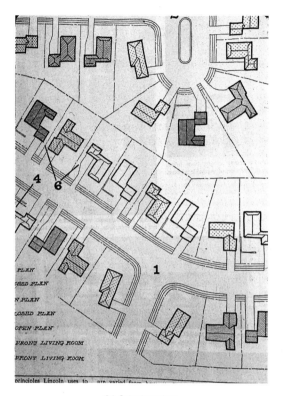

24 *Suburban plans*

Planned Assaults

Thirty years later American suburban planners have begun to prune the gird, to create Pope's "ladders," where each fork in the road ends in a cul-de-sac, literally stopping all flows, all movement, all promenades. This attack on the grid as universal access for all has diagrammatic similarities to the Plan Obus, although isolation rather than consolidation is the intent. The cell stacked along a multidimensional axis in the Obus has been exchanged for the suburban house, strung like beads along the cul-de-sac streets. Having replaced the perimeter block as the basic building block, a totem of the American Dream, the single-family house is fundamental to the rethinking of the metropolis. But it is not merely a footprint on the metropolitan surface but its microcosm, its very model.

Underlying the work is thus the assumption that the single-family house is a "disciplinary mechanism," morality manifested in form. The assignment of rooms, furniture, and equipment, and their syntax, is a vehicle of ideology and a behavioral modifier. The built form is supported by numerous additional structures of influence: the rhetoric of politics and law, ceremonial oratory, the language of everyday life, and various texts and image assemblies, from the codes of behavior whose sources range from the advice columns and advertising to television soap operas.[10]

Corbusian plans, sections, technology, and oratory have come a long way in suburbia. Rarely have we seen a more effective culture-shaping assembly of devices. Using seemingly benign and timid "technologies" and invisible propaganda methods rather than Corbusian bombast has proven a most effective way to drive the suburban complex of lifestyle and real estate machine.

25 *Opera*
Photograph from the exhibition "The Eichler Homes: Building the California Dream,"
University of Texas, Austin, 1998.

In the 1950s Joseph L. Eichler, a housing developer, presented a modern suburban house to the booming market in California. Unlike most other suburban developers, Eichler used architects (Quincy Jones, Frederick Emmons, Anshen and
Allen, and Claude Oakland) to create strikingly modern houses, overdetermined by
an equally modern lifestyle projected through photography and advertising
brochures. The architectural homunculus is no longer Corbu's new man but the
family: parents and children presented in a circle—a *life cycle*—around the kitchen
counter that, not coincidentally, concentrically spreads dining and living around
food preparation. Similarly each family member is housed in rooms around a cen-

tral atrium: the twenty-four-hour life cycle. A cycle that needs no utopia but the firm belief in family values and procreation to survive. The photographs by Ernest Braun of the model Eichler family of the middle 1950s appear operatic today in their unfettered and naïve enthusiasm. They represent one of the few successful attempts to bring the architect to the suburban housing market, and as such must remain in our focus.

26 *Assaults*
The single-family home: poised for intervention.

My first employment in the United States was as a draftsman in Claude Oakland's office in San Francisco, working on the last generation of Eichler houses. The year was 1966. My obsession with suburbia, its houses and plans, may have begun there. Although motivated and inspired by Eichler's project, I was deeply skeptical of the propagandistic and manipulative advertising of the suburban life cycle. I began a cycle of work, the *planned assaults* on the single-family house. Clearly an expression of my ambiguous conscience, the work was also the ground for a lasting research on what had already proved to be the ambiguous relations between subjects and objects, on distraction and absorption.[11]

My position on the two extremes of Benjamin's conceptualization has always come down on the side of ambiguity and the need for action on the part of the dweller. Most architects seem to ignore the dilemma, and leave the problem of architectural relevance to the user. James Stirling's position on the subject, as manifested in his Stuttgart Staatsgalerie of 1985, is not evasive but pragmatic, populist if you will. The relationship between Schinkel's Altes Museum and Stirling's Stuttgart addition is well known. A large U-shaped fragment of the old enfilade of rooms from the museum in Berlin is almost reconstructed in the addition. But simultaneously, a public pedestrian link is laid across the galleries in the shape of a giant ramp much like the ramp in Corbu's Carpenter Center of 1963. With postmodernist bravura and informality Stirling combines the world of the enfilade with that of the architectural promenade, closing the circle, possibly suggesting that one is just the extension of the other. More potently, Stirling has manifested Benjamin's dichotomy of distraction and concentration by giving the strolling public their own path across the museum, lightly brushing by its demanding displays of art, and also by giving the enfilade back to the art aficionado who in the backwater of the swift river of the city can concentrate on the displays undisturbed. Like Alexander, Stirling severed the Gordian knot with one swift chop. We have again come to the end of the promenade, but unlike our encounter with the end at the solarium on the roof of the Villa Savoye, this is the conceptual end (although Stirling's promenade actually connects with the entire street system of the city). The promenade is finite, a mere prosthetic device that meets needs of a particular kind, presented on equal terms with the enfilade. It holds no false promises about the future. Stripped of its utopia and Corbusian pathos, the promenade has become just another technology left in the graveyard of modernism—another place to hurry through. Unfortunately, the pragmatic tactic of providing an outlet both for distraction and for absorption does not bring us closer to the center of my inquiry.

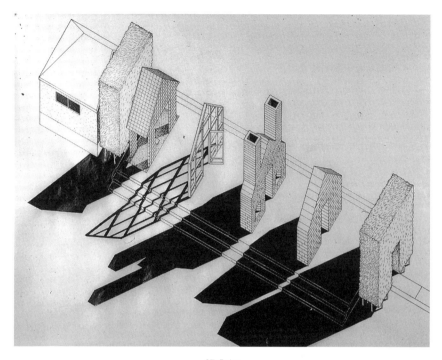

27 *Delay*
Villa Prima Facie, axonometric, Lars Lerup, 1985.

Walter Benjamin writes: "Around 1840 it was briefly fashionable to take turtles for a walk in the arcades. The *flâneurs* liked to have the turtles set the pace for them. If they had had their way, progress would have been obliged to accommodate itself to this pace. But this attitude did not prevail; Taylor [American and father of scientific management, a method that led Ford to revolutionize car production], who popularized the watchword 'Down with dawdling!' carried the day."[12] The *flâneur,* or dandy—possibly the inventor of the concept of leisure—attempted to slow the pace of the rushing crowd that went about its everyday life to the beat of scientific management, much like cogs in a machine. The turtle served as a delay of the everyday narrative and its inevitable end. And, as Benjamin realized, the aesthetic strategy to end the mad rush of time was miserably defeated.

Villa Prima Facie (A House at First Appearance), of 1975, is the first attempt to interfere in the suburban realm, by designing a house that explicitly delays the everyday narrative. As with Benjamin's *flâneur,* the turtle is the house. According to the client, the new house should remind him as little as possible of the master bedrooms and living rooms of his past. Therefore, the stereotypical plan is erased and a tabula rasa (in the modernist spirit?) is created, on which a series of walls is placed in enfilade. Each wall is an independent element rather than a part of a room. These soft, dry, hot, hard, and wet walls are finally sheltered by a greenhouse. Highly descriptive of its condition, each wall attempts to slow down the everyday narrative. Such a slowing down would only come with collusion, with a desire on the part of the dweller to let himself be absorbed. Activities associated with the separate walls, such as the regular clipping of the topiary soft wall, or the reading by the dry wall while the rain patters on the greenhouse, or the daily shower under the wet wall, are all delays that slow down and attenuate everyday life, much as a description would in a literary narrative. The promenade hovers surreptitiously in the openings cut in each of the walls, hinting at the future beyond. When reached, however, the end is a bedroom—the little sleep—far from the Corbusian utopia.

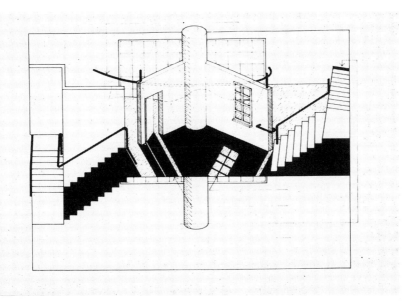

28 *Traps*
The Liberated Handrail, the Useless Door, the Fresh Window, the Stair That Leads Nowhere.
Nofamily House, from Lars Lerup, *Planned Assaults*, 1987.

The Nofamily House of 1978–1981 is designed for a stereotypical family whose everyday narrative is juxtaposed on a house filled with traps set to delay or completely stop it. A Liberated Handrail ceases at one point to serve its dull assignment, abandoning its use value to simply revel in its form. A Useless Door stares accusingly at its user, while the Fresh Window allows a new point of view on family life. Finally, the Stair That Leads Nowhere stops the architectural promenade just at the ceiling, prohibiting a Corbusian conclusion at a potential solarium. Aside from Corbu and Benjamin, the inspirations are Duchamp and his coat hanger nailed to the floor, causing everyone to trip, and the atmosphere of frustration and endless delay described by Jorge Luis Borges in "The Immortal" of 1956:

> A labyrinth is a structure compounded to confuse men; its architecture,
> rich in symmetries, is subordinated to that end. In the palace the archi-

tecture lacked any such finality. It abounded in deadended corridors, high unattainable windows, portentous doors which led to a cell or pit, incredible inverted stairways whose steps and balustrades hung downwards. Other stairways, clinging airily to the side of a monumental wall, would die without leading anywhere, after making two or three turns in the lofty darkness of the cupolas.[13]

As Umberto Eco has pointed out in his *Theory of Semiotics,* the Russian formalists were fond of using the so-called "device of making it strange," *priem ostrannenja,* in an attempt to increase the "difficulty and the duration of the perception, of the art object itself"—the text becomes self-focusing: it directs the attention of the addressee primarily to its own shape.[14] This is an attempt to overcome the chasm between Benjamin's "distraction and concentration" and bring subject and object closer together.

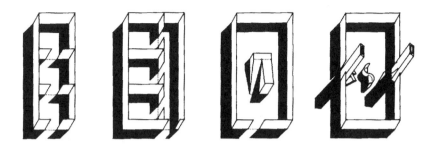

29 *A Plan Degree Zero*
Three plans: enfilade, corridor, and free, and a postmodern coda: the Plan Degree Zero; Lars Lerup, 1989.

During 1989 a house was designed for four clients: two women with their young sons. The house was to be set in the Garden District in New Orleans. An offspring of the Texas Zero, the New Zero creates a neutral plane—a *plan degree zero*. Unlike the Corbusian *plan libre,* the neutral plane does not promise freedom but establishes a status quo: a genteel version of Borges's palace. This neutrality is achieved by using a common rhetorical device called reversion, exemplified in the statement:

"He has, has he?"

The statement is formally symmetrical across the comma but the meaning is not; "has he?" puts the first assertion in question and therefore turns the sentence in upon itself, creating a neutrality or status quo. The plan of the New Zero is full of these figures: two Leaning Fireplaces (one in compression, the other in tension), the Which-Way-Mirror, the Sofa/Bed, the Which-Way-Chair, the First Worktable/Last Supper Table, and the Almost Symmetrical Kitchen-Toilet-Bathroom Houses. Assembled in "sentences," the components form reversions and in other cases palindromes ("sentences" that read the same forward and backward).[15] The idea of a territory degree zero is mediated by the interest in "the enfilade of rooms," "the double-loaded corridor plan," and the "free plan." From this stems at first the Plan Degree Zero, in which ambiguous furniture demands that the dweller construct her own paths and fields. The ambiguity consists in double meanings: sofa and bed, last supper and table. The ambiguous furniture leads in turn to the Household Vehicles, where the dweller can see her own subject as a shadow/automaton. The key is to embrace movement, the "forking of paths" (Borges), the "movable feast" (Steinbeck), while double meanings prevail: sofa/bed/coffin, closet/coffin, chair/wheelbarrow, bookcase/library ladder (fig. 43).

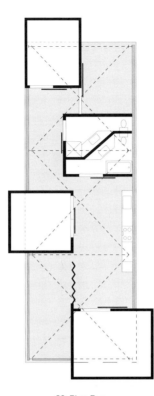

30 *River Run*
or the House That Roars; Lars Lerup, 1998.

In 1998, to date the last iteration of the neutral plane, a further articulation of the plan was made, as a river of activity interspaced by eddies of rooms. Metaphorically, I exchanged the *life cycle* for the *river of life*, suggesting that life despite procreation does not repeat itself but goes on while transforming and changing. The plan with its riverlike serpentine also provides eddies or rooms that in ensemble create levels of privacy, ranging from total to partial. The stereotypical arrangement of living, dining, and cooking is abandoned or negated, although the equipment may still be present. The aim is to make a world of form and formality, but with minimal suggestions for use. This reinforces that the relation between dwellers and architecture must be acted upon because fundamentally ambiguous.

31 *Ambiguity*

Ambiguity and Action

There is a distinct distance between the body and the marching rooms of the en-filade. Here the walls lived separate from the pedestrian, whose only reflection is the outline of the doors. This clarity of distinction between the human and the artificial is completely abandoned in the architectural promenade that serves as a prosthetic device for the new man—surreptitiously we slip from the realm of flesh and blood to the world of artifice. No wonder that we have begun to confuse ourselves with it, and call for more anthropomorphic semblance. Yet this is a fool's errand. There are shades of schizophrenia and megalomania in this confusion of self and world. The confusion is most apparent in the insistence that architecture is representative of us, when by now, after so many years of internal formation, architecture must be seen as a parallel enterprise, whose relationship with us is always ambiguous, *until we act on it*.

In the 1980s historicism led many architects to return to columns, porticos, and, alas, broken pediments. These devices attempted to create ambiguity by putting the structure of the building into (some) question. Returning briefly to the hypothesis that there are only two kinds of plans, the enfilade and the corridor-generated, I would like to propose a new hypothesis: there are three kinds of plans, to the former two adding the *plan libre* and in particular its postmodern version that I have called the neutral plane and the associated technologies of delay and ambiguity. This is a new dimension of the communication between the subject, its mind and body, and architecture.

Hope cannot be severed from architecture, even if at this time it must be found inside architecture: there is a fork at the end of the promenade. In assuming the position of a fictional character of Borges, the new plan for the suburban house takes a position. Borges writes and Ts'ui Pen speaks:

> *I leave the various futures (not all) to my garden of forking paths.* In all fictional works, each time a man is confronted with several alternatives, he chooses one and eliminates the others; in the fiction of Ts'ui Pen, he chooses—simultaneously—all of them. He creates, in this way, diverse futures, diverse times which themselves also proliferate and fork.[16]

It is in a new suburban house that the first steps toward a new metropolis must be taken, and it is in this "garden of forking paths" that the dweller in thought and action must find his or her freedom.

32 *Action*
From *room,* an installation by Lars Lerup and Sohela Farohki, The Menil Collection, 1999.

Words are . . . like ice. . . . And, if poets struggle against the iciness of words and refuse to fall into the traps set by signs, it is ever more appropriate that architects should conduct a comparable campaign, for they have at their disposal both materials analogous to signs (bricks, wood, steel, concrete) and material analogous to those "operations" which link signs together, articulating them and conferring meaning upon them (arches, vaults, pillars, and columns; openings and enclosures; construction techniques; and the conjunction and disjunction of such elements). Thus it is that architectural genius has been able to realize spaces dedicated to voluptuousness (the Alhambra of Granada), to contemplation and wisdom (cloisters), to power (castles and chateaux) or to heightened perception (Japanese gardens). Such genius produces spaces full of meaning, spaces which first and foremost escape mortality: enduring, radiant, yet also inhabited by a specific local temporality. Architecture produces living bodies, each with its own distinctive traits. The animating principle of such a body, its presence, is neither visible nor legible as such, nor is it the object of any discourse, for it reproduces itself within those who use the space in question, within their lived experience. Of that experience the tourist, the passive spectator, can grasp but a pale shadow.[17]

Although deeply ambiguous, the relation between subjects and objects will take productive form through collusion and action. As I suggested in *Building the Unfinished* of 1977, the dweller must act in order to see. Architecture comes alive in action. Theoretically the concept of architecture as a verb was nurtured in the phenomenology of Merleau-Ponty, who wrote (still) mysteriously:

To look at an object is to inhabit it. . . . Our previous formula must . . . be modified: the house itself is not the house seen from nowhere, but the house seen from everywhere. The completed object is translucent, being shot through from all sides by an infinite number of present scrutinies which intersect in its depth leaving nothing hidden.[18]

And later, the more pragmatic and practical thinking of George Herbert Mead and my very senior colleague Herbert Blumer, whose words still resound: "When in doubt, go out and look." During the 1980s, the era of formalist obsession in architecture, it was my stubbornness that kept my own version of interactionism alive. For me, it is still the dynamic and elusive in-between separating and holding together subjects and objects that drives my project.

All uses require space, and as long as there is use there is the potential for architecture. As architects we are not only agents of its use but agents of its making, a role that Lefebvre doesn't cover but that gives dual quality to an architecture school, since many miniature spaces are created inside the body of the school—in its studios and computers. Think of how many small projects students have designed and built (as models). Think of them as pools of energy, buoying and lifting us out of the morass of the mundane, onto a plane of creativity, innovation, skill, ambition, and pleasure. We are the custodians of this energy, which if used wisely will flow out into the world and spawn numerous architectural bodies, which in turn will be brought alive by use. This is an awesome thought that gives tremendous value to our profession: *we help build living bodies*. The French theorist Michel de Certeau put it somewhat differently: "To walk is to lack a place."[19] To Houstonians who move mostly by car, the sense of "lack of place" is greatly heightened. After all, pedestrians don't feel as if the buildings they walk along move, especially since most cities made for pedestrians have continuous buildings lining the sidewalks. But Houston drivers, in the face of all reason, see the world fly by, thus revving up the sense of placelessness. If in addition the driver leaves a generic office space behind, to arrive at a house almost identical to the neighbors', only the other mates or members of the family, their heirlooms, and the personal effects help slow down the sense of "always going west."

Place, argues de Certeau, is a "configuration of stable positions," while *space* "is like the word when it is spoken."[20] Thus the drivers of the freeway are involved in making space while simultaneously leaving place behind in the dust. These long, attenuated spaces form invisible cocoons that come alive every time the driver gets on the road. Yet the connection between place and space is intimate, since de Certeau also argues that "space is a practiced place." Place does not exist until it is practiced or turned into space. We are back to the construction of everyday life. This finally suggests that while lacking place we are simultaneously performing place, making placelessness in Houston a somewhat less urgent problem. Lefebvre and de Certeau put enormous weight and value on the role of the dweller in the awakening of architecture and place. Use, in turn, propelled by the dweller, is a key to this complexity.

Use, in all its splendid complexity (by the way, far beyond what we normally understand as the program), brings this energy forth, and numerous *stims* are lit across the plains, along mountainsides, in valleys, in cities, in neighborhoods. We can choose to sulk over the fact that there seems to be little appreciation of this awesome thought, but we can also choose to take it in our own hands and bring it forth to the world. As Lefebvre says: "its presence is neither visible nor legible as such, nor is it the object of any discourse."[21] This puts an enormous burden on us, since to live this awesome thought you must build the body. We are caught in a paradox: the society that pays for our services has forgotten (or much more likely, has never experienced) the power of the living body of architecture, yet we have to build it to convince them.[22] Here our convictions will be put to test, and our skills of persuasion. To convince the world will be at least as hard as it is to build that magical body.

The Metropolitan Architect

Architects' Hands

In a photograph of Louis I. Kahn, his hand, closer to the camera and therefore proportionally larger, frames his face, to dominate in two ways. The photograph renders Kahn speechless, allowing the hand its prominence by size and position. Held halfway between him and us, Kahn's hand heralds his profession, constructing a mythic bond between the architect's imagination and his work. Straying from the customary center of an architect's words and work, it signals an occasion to enter a panoramic speculation about architects' hands, ostensibly to let certain myths of mastery slip away and to contemplate instead some of the body's propensities.[23]

Kahn's hand is wide open. An open mouth, the hand is empty yet full of expression. The simile drawn between hand and mouth may not just be rhetorical. Biologists have speculated that the complex similarity between the opposing thumb and the larynx is the trace of the emergence of speech, giving the concept of body language new meaning. Kahn's open hand is not the carpenter's or the mason's hand, normally implied in architects' hands by professional propinquity, but a hand emptied, liberated from the labors of construction—free from the pencil and the T-square even. But all the rhetorical bombast is muted by the photographic silence, and the hand-in-gesture springs forth as a promise: not of a building but of the *built in use*; a synoptic liaison of object and subject, of form and will. As such, architecture is but a bleak facsimile of the hand. In the hand lies the ultimate dream of an *architecture vivante,* an architecture *alive.*

Today, as illustrated hands go, those of architects are no longer in focus. Gone are professional hands in gesture: hands holding architectural models, pencils, or cigarettes (for affect and style). Instead hands are held close to the body, hiding in pockets or like soft crutches propping up (weary) heads. Hands appear in other places, disembodied, fleeting, mere synecdoches of human presence, or more interestingly as shadows, as contact prints on machines: on their levers—as in computer mice, remote control devices, or (on Sundays at the shooting range) precision rifle butts.

Inside the machine, in its working parts, in its very intelligence, even the hand's shadow is nearly forgotten. "These machines . . . are our best wishes for our hands," writes Charles Siebert, describing his father's affection for old tool-and-die devices. In the end, "even these old machines were too complex." In describing them, his father "was reduced to miming the various motions by which each one, with its mounted precision tool, shapes a piece of metal against a molded die."[24] As in work at the machine, in description the hands are reduced to miming the very machine they instigated, and worse, to miming a machine that in turn was the mere re-creation of the labor of those same hands. The operative word here is not mime but *reduced,* since to my mind it is not the hands that have been reduced but the machines. Hand surgeons and robotics engineers can attest to this. Hands still hold an enormous secret—a complex intelligence whose description has yet to see the light.

In industrial labs, particularly in the silicon alleys and valleys of the world, hands are either in the way of or on the way to computers. From high-five recognition systems, hand gestures that "tell" machines what to do, keyboards, electronic pencils, to direct-hand interventions, hands are still doing a lot of the walking. But the flows and signals do not travel one way. In his *User's Guide to the Millennium,* J. G. Ballard implies that machines are powerful, mesmerizing, but that their feedbacks, however faint, reveal sinister limitations:

> *Typewriter* It types *us*, encoding its own linear bias across the free space of the imagination.[25]

A typewriter, before its reinvention as a machine, referred to the person "writing" the type. Subsequently, the typewriter came to "write" the operator, but now, in spite of the keyboard, the linear bias is not fully carried over to the computer. Thanks to the new writing program's editing capabilities, the writer is now in a field whose linear furrows can be arrested, retraced, erased, displaced, and reversed. The almost-free space of the imagination? Probably not, just a new and possibly more subtle type of bondage. Now the hand hovers above and below the keyboard: the digital (as in the digits of the hands) and the binary (as in the computer's 0's and 1's). The hands' ten digits are now capable of a digital complexity that very few of us will ever comprehend. Yet, in this new play of digits, "does the body exist at all," and, as Ballard goes on to ask, "will it accept its diminished role?"[26] After all, our hands are typing with all ten digits, yet their message gets collapsed into the two index-digits (at least in the computer below the keys). Will the remaining eight gather their peculiarities (pinkie/lazy, ring/fidelity, middle/rude, thumb/happy) and start a rebellion? No longer just a working tool or symbol, the hand reemerges full-fledged. No longer with all its tricks up the sleeve, but right here and now, our hands will operate the complete "digital" menu with dizzying biotechnic wizardry, with bit for bit coincidence in a parallel universe. Until now, the hand designing our various universes (modernist, postmodern, deconstructive, minimalist) has been far from parallel, but constrained, colonized, and held down by the universe itself. With lighter touch, more ease, more directness, more parallelism, other universes will appear dexterous, liquid, and alive.

If "science fiction is the body's dream of becoming a machine," are our hands-in-gesture the body's dream of becoming architecture?[27] Is there something more in Kahn's hand than the architect's calling card or the stylization of some great architectural event? Is the new hand less the puppet in the theater of technology than that of the puppeteer herself, a biotechnology serving to spawn one of the million nano-tsunamis of the metropolis?

Symbolically, Kahn's hand has lost its authority, its status as a model and a promise of a highly evolved architecture in which form and will are inseparable. Simultaneously with the decline of authority, Kahn as the master has lost some of his luster too. Now the open hand gapes over a loss.

The era is gone "when cathedrals were white" (Le Corbusier) and still held their citizens in subdued awe with their muffled dramas in a single ironclad perspective (Bataille). Monumental architecture has become media events of brief social consequence. Mass education is slowly unsettling authority, expertise, privilege, and even authorship. Although still star-struck, architects have joined the ranks of product designers who in team efforts produce designs of no clear pedigree or single origin. Even under the banner of a single star designer, as everyone knows, the office has become a nebula whose inner workings are so complex and dispersed that the author is effectively decentered, if not dead. Spawned and buoyed by this non-hierarchical inertia, swarms of new interests may soon be moving toward unorganized coincidence: a democracy of hands making a new metropolitan space.

The search for a new metropolitan architecture just beyond the traditional grasp of the hand of the master is fraught with entanglements and opportunities. Kenneth

Frampton's compelling call for a regional architecture may well work in a distinct lo-cale with considerable cultural character and depth, but in the metropolis the sur-face is beckoning. Metropolitan architecture must be the interplay between this surface and the depth of a specific place. This binary proposition is deceptively sim-ple. The two axes, the local and the global, are hopelessly intertwined and each in themselves vast and unwieldy. Paring down and parsing is necessary.

My research on the plan of the suburban house is an inner search. But this in-teriority is not about the depth of a locale but about the metropolitan surface—about the general state of the average modern family—a stereotype that sweeps through all metropolises. Diagrams of habits and mores, these plans must find their depth in place at the time of their realization. Like great wines, the plans must find their *terroir*: the complex fusion of weather, climate, and soil as fostered by the at-tentive hands of the winemaker. It is in this vein that we must understand the "grow-ing of our houses."

The Architect's House

The struggle between the homely desire and the global push and pull of the surface is the site for metropolitan architecture. Albert Frey, the Swiss architect trans-planted to the high California desert on the outskirts of greater Los Angeles, may have instinctively understood this complex site before anyone else. His two houses in Palm Springs stand in their lightness and in their unsentimental tribute to nature and modern technology as touchstones of metropolitan habitation.

Like a pilot in a treacherous ship channel, Frey navigates so elegantly between the modern techniques of the time and the ancient site with its huge boulders and grand vistas as to take my breath away. Looking from an eagle's perspective at a corner of his last house, I see a rusted corrugated roof, two open sliding doors and a dimpled white duvet on a bed, desert, concrete, and the mirroring of a portion of the swimming pool.[28] The colors travel across nature and culture. The surrounding jagged rocks of geological catastrophe gently protest the rationalized corrugations of the metal roof. The desert wind is sweet with wildflowers.

Not a car or an Airstream, hermetically closed in on themselves, Frey's work is not about technical domination. Nor is the work about nature-pandering, although it reaches out to nature with hot desire. The house and nature remain incomplete.

Both will miss Frey: his asceticism, his determined habits, the lack of furniture, the abundance of storage, his grasp of the land's grandeur. This is habitation, a focus that when lost ends up in gadgetry and other forms of fetishism. There is no sense of dogma. Habitation can take as many forms as there are individuals seeking freedom. Panoramic, the inside, the outside, the surface of the desert metropolis, and the depth of this unique place are manifested, built, and held in focus.

The Architect in the Metropolis

In a photograph of 1995, Frey stands in his house looking out at the panorama beyond the frame. Thin, ethereal, his long knotty hands rest. One hand is spread out on his right leg, the other barely touching a table. An architect's table? His body is curved against the table, and the arm, hand, and table make a third leg of a tripod. Grounded, the metropolitan architect has very sharp dark eyes. He no longer needs the architect's aura; he has become the fulcrum of the two axes, place and extent.

He stands, presumably unaware, at the edge of a new metropolitan space, a space that does not suffer from name, place, or time, a hyperreality in which we "see" all people, all facades, and the entire interior at the same time (Borges's Aleph).[29] Hallucinatory for now, yes, but perhaps not for long. The ultradynamic simultaneity of the twenty-four-hour metropolis is already demanding a new spatial awareness for itself. The work of Kahn, Frey, and others has been repossessed and reconfigured and is now effectively consolidated in the genetics of the metropolis. Let the intense solar wind from the metropolis illuminate and gather all exemplary design under its own auspices.

Hesitation

In Frey's desert house I sense a longing, a gap that can only be mended by habitation's own desire. This speculation is predicated on the house, the site, and Frey's body language—the parallel between body and language—between the *reason* of language and the *gestures* of the body. In pantomime, the body reasons, but more unsettling, language can also mime the body—who is to know? Deleuze, whose century we are soon leaving,[30] suggests that the mixed messages from body and language stem from the repeated *hesitation* built into the workings of body and reason. Thoughts proceed in "fits and starts," just as an end of an arm decides to be a hand before it knows whether it is the left and right hand. In earlier work I thought of this hesitation as *the unfinished*, and *to build the unfinished* as habitation proper. Taken in two ways, the unfinishedness refers to the dynamic binding by the dweller to the physical setting, and to the setting itself, always in the making. The addition of hesitation suggests an inherent blindness or unpredictability superadded to the unfinished. How many times have I seen my plans designing "another" house, my writing constructing its own reason, or my body stumbling over itself? These potential bifurcations threaten reason itself, while liberating both language and body.

The unsettling of reason and the enigma of pantomime allow the appearance of an abundance of marginalities. Deleuze calls them *phantasms*.[31] Be they theological, oneiric, or erotic, our hands have performed them all: the believer crossing himself, the hands as the body's dream of architecture, the clandestine hand seeking a site to perform the unmentionable. Despite his groundedness, this is the space Frey stands at the edge of, our future space. Speculations about this future must retain its unfinishedness, its hesitations. In the end all hands are probably not copies of reason but simulacra of the surface, parts of a Dionysian machine that when allowed to wander and to fabricate will free us from our imagined destinies.[32]

Work

The hero is dead, but what about the thousand others, those in line and those on other trajectories? The atomization of life, technology, work, and entertainment and the simultaneous upward centralization of economic power produce a peculiar glitch—a zone of rapid change, filled with potential freedom and its opposite. The struggle over control of the new infrastructures—network computing, telephony, cable television, and energy, to mention the most important—is a reflection of the struggle of the many with the few. A thousand designers hunkered down over their computer screens are amongst the many, and they have the potential to change their profession, dramatically! Women and men: the sheer volume of talented well-trained designers now flooding the market, occupying every empty seat in the drafting halls, is a power that could fundamentally alter the map of metropolitan culture. The odds are awkward. On the one hand the chances of becoming a signature architect are worse than the lottery. (In each sizable country there are only a few seats at the high table, and only one in smaller ones—a Siza in Portugal, a Rossi in Italy, a Nouvel in France.) And on the other hand, the chance of remaining amongst the rank and file is high because it may be the most comfortable choice.

Yet the sheer collective power of mind, talent, and know-how among the un-known designers is immense.[33] Unknown designers moonlight. Clandestinely or accidentally they design high quality into otherwise mundane commercial projects, assist and make possible the work of master architects, design outside the narrow confines of the profession, construct thousands of houses, additions, and refur-bishings for families expecting mere commodity, while thousands of others go on thinking and dreaming.

All this activity would have occurred unnoticed in the past, but this time it may be different. The new communication channels, with their chat groups, web pages, and e-mail traffic, will lead to network enterprise,[34] in which professionals gather around specific projects like tow trucks around a freeway accident. Design coali-tions may take time to form, since clients demand predictability (traditionally held by well-established firms). Here recent developments around virtuality may change attitudes toward predictability, since virtual buildings may allow not only a visit to your future office or apartment but entry into a design process in which dwellers at the outset gather with all the actors in the process from conception to sale. And with designers becoming savvier in accessing capital (and with network capitalists traveling the same networks), network firms may soar. Simultaneously, and now more spontaneously, once the micropowers of design begin to throttle through our new highways, unorganized coincidence may occur and design will well up from the floor of the metropolis. Dispersed, miniaturized, and unauthorized in the literal sense—a cultural inundation—new patterns of design may emerge on vastly dif-ferent scales. The metropolis will finally have its own design culture. Just as the city and architecture (as we have known it since the Renaissance) are disappearing be-cause of the atomization of the metropolis and its manifold technologies, these new micropowers, after their divide-and-conquer, will manifest themselves, fleetingly to be sure, and maybe only as patterns, proliferations, disjointed speech, haptic ca-dences and events; and only occasionally as traditional, comprehensible built form, because motivated by new vision machines, or because of sheer numbers and the muscle of repetition.

The change needed, for a discipline and profession that have labored in the shadow of the master architect, is radical and will require a thorough conceptual revamping, a revamping that includes all actors from designers to dwellers. Robert

Goodman wrote in his 1971 *After the Planners*: "By raising the possibilities of a humane way of producing places to live, by phasing out the elitist nature of environmental professionalism, we can move toward a time when we will no longer define ourselves by our profession, but by our freedom as people."[35] The conceptual step from distributed design to new engagements in the re-creation of the metropolis by the dwellers is not far. Distant in time but not in possibility, Goodman's fighting words are still with us.

Attempts to redress the dispersal by reorganizing have ranged from Frank Lloyd Wright's Broadacre City[36] to the Goodman brothers' *Communitas*,[37] straddling the political spectrum from right to left. The proposals are characterized by an ambivalent acceptance of the suburban, and by attempts to reurbanize. Ironically, the much-maligned metropolis, with its strip malls, sprawl, and apparent disorganization, may be harboring a new democratic force that will lead to massive (erratic), widespread freedom and upgrades in environmental quality.

Value

Turning away from the city toward the metropolis also means turning toward new data. The data needed to build the old city were bound to building and its immediate externalities. Enhanced and propelled by new technologies, metropolitan data are vastly different. They are no longer bounded but, like the metropolis itself, wide, scattered, and unwieldy. The amount and variety of data are further complicated by the sense that design can no longer rely on traditional building data but must now be opened to "all." The general output of metropolitan data is Babelian in its incomprehensibility, leaving vast mounds at the feet of modern managers and designers. What does it all mean? How can the data be enhanced and be made informative? How can sheer weight become intelligence?

Architects have always had to act under uncertainty, even when the data were confined to the city. This was done as a matter of course; design action solved the dilemma. The catastrophic shift from data to synthesis had a built-in transformational step in which data were deemed unimportant or made informative and turned into synthesis. This ability to discriminate and conceptualize is needed more than ever, and architects may be better prepared than most. The challenge lies in accepting the Babelian nature of the information at hand, and in beginning to parse it to make manageable and finite elements that, combined, can build the new metropolis.

The key in the transformation of metropolitan data is to focus on the purpose. Why and how does a better physical setting enhance our lives? How does it add *value*? Architects' tendency to leave the determination of value outside their professional realm, relying on architecture's history and reputation, is hopelessly antiquated. A far more aggressive attitude toward architecture as a real value is sorely needed. Money and cost will invariably enter the equation, but they have become part of the infrastructure. To think that architects still cannot "come in on budget," with all the available techniques of cost control, is mystifying. In fact, cost as a concept, even the creation of wealth, must be superseded by value. This is no small matter, since it is clear that postwar architects have not been able to articulate the complex value of good design.

The crisis of value in design has surreptitiously moved architecture toward becoming a consumer good. The housing market in Houston is a prime example of this "degradation." Here location and cost are the only parameters of design, provided that the house is a Georgian. To prove to this jaded, uninspired market that a modern house—a modern environment—bound to the two axes of the metropolis is of value requires a major campaign that has yet to find its movers and shakers, not to speak of its audience.

Ilya Prigogine, the Nobel laureate physicist and systems analyst, writes: "There need no longer be a gap between the 'hard' sciences, which speak of certitudes, and the 'soft' sciences which deal with possibilities."[38] This is heartening, even if Prigogine's proof is for most of us inaccessible. It is lodged in the area of physics that he calls "irreversible processes,"[39] which in my crude interpretation suggests that all systems have emergent properties: those we used to think of as systems of certitude harbor possibility. Taking a risk, I suggest that this newly discovered possibility has positive bearing on the future of architecture.

Today, architects face the dual universe of certitude and possibility every time the developer tells them about the inflexibility and certitude of the bottom line. Invariably architects must back down because they are unable to equate the value of architecture with economic value. In fact, since the demise of modernism we have been patently unable to speak coherently about architecture's value, much less quantify it. Unless we are willing to face this challenge, I suggest that architecture will disappear, and with it our profession. Urgently we must unsettle the certitude of the bottom line by articulating architectural value in terms understandable by developers and clients at large.

Prigogine writes that as long as we have the same *arrow of time,* we have—in all aspects of existence from cosmology to psychology—complex amalgams of laws and events. And since events are always associated with bifurcation, with various possibilities, we have choices and thus values. Prigogine concludes that we must find "the narrow path between the deterministic world, which leads to alienation, and the random world," which would exclude human rationality and lead to utter chaos.[40]

To appreciate the task ahead, let me take a very simple example. Every spring term for fifteen years, I used to teach an introductory course at the University of California at Berkeley called "People and Environment." One of the most common and reasonable questions directed to me at the customary Socratic fifteen minutes after each lecture was: "What is architecture?" A question to which I answered variously. One of the more impudent answers was: "Any building that has ceiling heights over eight feet"—suggesting that anything above and beyond standard building practice was architecture. Let us now transfer this to a bottom line discussion in the developer's office, where architect A attempts to raise the ceilings to ten feet: "to give a sense of space," as she puts it. The developer groans and says that this would increase the current square foot cost from 115 dollars to 135 (assuming that to add one vertical foot at the ceiling adds roughly 10 dollars to the square foot cost). Now she is stumped, because architects do not know how to give a dollar value to the "sense of space." Simply put, architecture has no value at worst and esoteric value at best—value only in the eye of the beholder.

The unraveling of this standoff will take a major societal change. As Prigogine suggests, such a change coincides with major changes in the view of science, but I contend that it is easier to change our view of science than our value system. Mihaly Csikszentmihalyi, a psychologist, states our dilemma as follows:

> Now, it seems to me that values which are not based on expectations of some form of transcendence must, by default, be material values. For me, the interesting question is not why economic values are so powerful, but rather why the alternatives are so weak at this point in his-

tory. Why is there a vacuum of hope, and we are left with so little be-
sides material values?[41]

In research he had done in Chicago, he asked a number of respondents where
they would go for solace and interest in the city. They listed five locations: the Sears
Tower (then the tallest building in the world), O'Hare Airport (the gateway to the
world beyond), the lakeshore (the panorama of city and nature), Marshall Field (the
largest store in town), and the Art Institute (the palace of art). (Note that no sports
arenas or churches where chosen.) Csikszentmihalyi concluded that the respondents went to these places in *awe,* with a sense of pride, even transcendence.[42]

It should come as no great surprise that we have set aside transcendence for
the material. There was a time, particularly when we were worse off materially, when
religion, hope, and faith played a much more important role in our lives. Through
the systematic improvement of our material conditions we have come to realize that
we have considerable control of our destiny, rather than being at the whim of fate
or God's will. We can easily see how the literal transcendence of—the going
above—the eight-foot ceiling, at substantial material cost, is put in serious jeop-
ardy. However, I very much doubt that we will ever win the argument if we try to find
a dollar equivalent; instead we must begin the long and hard struggle to find a way
of comparing apples with oranges.

With the emergence of the material as the most important value, all other more
esoteric values have declined in importance. The turn toward predominantly material values has been a long historic process that may take equal time and commitment to change. This change of emphasis is an evolutionary process; in order to
bring weight back to transcendent values, we might turn to the nature of evolution
itself. Csikszentmihalyi suggests three aspects of evolution that should be looked
at: *variation, selection,* and *transmission.*[43]

Variation

Using the concept of *meme* (reproduction through imitation, i.e., in the most
generic sense, memory) developed by the biologist Richard Dawkin (*The Selfish
Gene*), Csikszentmihalyi suggests that *patterns of values* are formed and stored in
the human mind and transmitted through culture.[44] Memes help affect our values.
They do not exactly determine our values, but they direct and constrain them. A va-

riety of memes are thus somatically and socially produced and disseminated.

Selection

We have *progressively* selected material values over transcendent ones. Now we have to find a way of producing new memes that will replace the old ones. In selection, *attention* becomes a crucial concept, or as Michael O'Hare suggests, "the most valued scarce resource in human life."[45] By paying *attention* to material values, we select them over transcendent values that we pay *less attention* to. And if other values survive long enough, we will transmit the new memes to the next generation through teaching, repetition, and persistent attention.

Hence when architects give in to the demand of translating everything into material terms, we *stop attending* to the values of architecture that can never be measured in dollars. Consequently our first step is to begin talking again about the esoteric values of architecture to our clients. Architecture's value is not just material and economic, but cultural and existential. Only then will we begin to form memes that will begin to compete for attention with the solidly established material ones.

Transmission

Architects have a clear advantage in their quest to transmit a new meme, since we don't have to rely entirely on words. We have architectural form.

The proliferation of memes has in modern times increased at a mind-boggling rate, largely because of information technologies—extrasomatic devices—such as books and computers. We may need to see architecture as such an extrasomatic device, particularly during this period of transition from totally materialistic values to a new more variegated and nuanced value system. The remarkable characteristic of the hard- and software of computers is their *complexity*—a galaxy of differentiated subsystems all integrated into one box and its network. The potential of such an apparatus is that any of these differentiated systems may be appreciated by itself or in unison with others. Many of these subsystems may appear incompatible, yet their integration suggests they are not. The computer and its software may serve well as a model for a new value system. The salient terms here are *complexity, differentiation,* and *integration.*[46]

The crisis of value is making its own demand on architects' speech and form: architects must speak up and *think aloud in form*. More than ever, *built thought* is essential to architects' professional status, which distinguishes us from those agents that see building as mere real estate. Since such a transformation of values is a cultural enterprise, we need many allies that will help to construct these reproductive units of value and make them proliferate and course through the social body. New meme technologies must be fashioned integrating values ranging from the material to the transcendent. For architects this is a conscious construction along two trajectories: rhetoric and building—what the ancient Greeks called *lexis* and *praxis*. We shall now turn to praxis.

Vehicular Behavior: A Portfolio of Images

33

When *living* is erased from living room, the *Ur*-text of enclosure brings to the surface ancient freedoms, obscure,
itinerant, uncertain. Momentarily the *room* seems free.

Figures 33–41 are from *room,* an installation by Lars
Lerup and Sohela Farohki, The Menil Collection, 1999.

34

The persistent shadows of everyday life are replaced by a
penumbra, a chiaroscuro that fogs our predetermined
destinies in favor of an almost-perfect future—right before
le plus-que-parfait French tense of a more-than-perfect
future (Steiner).

35

Begun as stories of the sea told by summering
sjökaptener and *styrmän* from the *ljugarbänken* (liar's
bench) in Lerhamn (from whence my family name stems),
my aspirations for the *oceanic* were etched in lapis blue.
(Genetically backed by generations of mariners on my
grandmother's side.) *room* is one of these lapidary
imaginations.

36

Across the unfrozen *room*-field, potential destinies are in-
sinuated in the household vehicles. This mobility at the
hands, feet, and bodies of the *roomers* erupts in roaming.
Like lantern flies, mythically lit, joyriders cross the field to
build new traffic situations.

37

In the lulls of mobility, the pastures of this fieldroom, the technics of the interiors, yield other vistas. Vistas of the real: pollution, as in cows and burnt air, and the clumsy limits of springs and aluminum tubes. Suggesting that the limits are no longer walls but *conditions* (consequences of our imagined freedom) and *states of mind*: our avarice and our purported superiority.

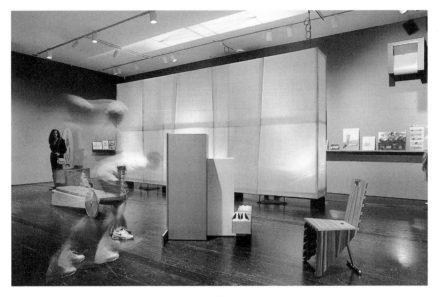

38

The instrumentality of the imaginary, as embedded in its startling tilting and the furious roar and crackle of the Wobbly Wall, rattles the everyday, humors our limitations, and throttles toward a future where everything moves, everything grows.

39

Swedish, English, and a passing knowledge of French, Italian, and German brought me to other polyglots—for warmth and camaraderie in the lack of a fixed linguistic ground. First Borges, then Beckett. In *room*, in this open field of multi-speak, the vehicles-in-motion are the speech acts. *room* is the ancient nomadic ground—a most American territory.

40

The three young drivers (at the moment of the camera shutter's abrupt (loud?) closure): what did they see? The hermeneutics of the objects, or their *thereness*—their exacting physicality? Their intended hilarity (Beckett)? Their hope? My yearning for a utopia? And most importantly, did they see the ethics? I will never know.

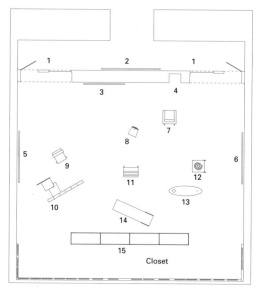

41

KEY

1: Rubber doors

2: Miasma 1

3: Miasma 4

4: Miasma 5

5: Miasma 6

6: Miasma 7

7: Racer

8: T

9: Watt's Lift

10: O'Meldon's Cube and Root

11: Tallboy

12: Lean-to

13: Maus 2

14: Flatbed

15: Wobbly Wall

Plan of *room* installation at the Menil Foundation, Houston.

Design Machines

Mechanisms of Closeness

Street crossings are walled off, people line the edge of the street, constructing with the buildings a city wall, half artifice, half human flesh. The bull, tightly surrounded by horses and riders leaning up against him, careens down this instant semi-soft boulevard—fear and courage. Embedded, larded in horse and human flesh, the bull is the motor of an ensemble of man-tool-animal—riders, horses, bull, and riding gear: stirrups, bits, and saddles. Leaning in on the bull, restraining him, a machine is formed through a morphing of flesh and technology. Sticking together, shape against shape, touching, softly deforming each other, the bond is the index. This new beast is benign when controlled but always dangerous, always ready to break its bonds, always ready to fall apart. Breaking loose, the bull pushes the horses and their riders apart, and dives into the soft wall—it screams. In the next instant the human wall scatters into individual agents scurrying, leaping, jumping to safety: Feria de Nîmes.

The assembly of men, horses, and bull careening down the makeshift bull run is a *design machine*. The assembly displays an understanding of men, their rituals, and animals—the result of a profoundly realistic and pragmatic analysis of a narrow reality. Simultaneously, without any break the same assembly is a design, in which mechanisms of closeness (using friction and force) are precariously assembled to form a momentary unity. This unity, this interactivity, is essential here. It is also a generic feature of design machines since it establishes the necessary relationships between all of their components: technical, human, and in this case animal. The assembly is a spatial flow—a space/time/economy fragment, in which there is only a figural distinction between rider and ride, between men and animal, between technology and flesh, between energy and waste, between opportunity-cost and desire. A spatial flow with a strict economy, an efficient use of material and resources: a beginning, a middle (the most harmonious part), and a potentially catastrophic

42 *Wet Machine*

end. As in Francis Bacon's *Novum Organum*[47] of 1620, the scene is an instrument of knowledge, but also a design: a machinic assembly and a pagan event with ancient roots in the struggle between men and animals, here almost harmoniously resolved. Even the time span between the perfect union of men and animals and the instant when the bull breaks the proximity is poignant: designs no longer last forever. This realization necessitates the understanding of the recovery phase—the bull must go back in the pen—a type of recycling. This is the life, productivity, and demise of *wet machines*. No longer machines of the mechanical kind, but rather the new kind in which the pulse of the driver is in direct parallel with the pulse of the animal, the strength of material, the tension in the harness and the stirrup, the interest and passion of the audience, the tenacity of the ritual institution of bullfights *à la camarguaise*.

The bull's breakout shatters, for a moment, the proximity grouping of man-tool-[animal]-machine-thing, and a transformation takes place. The bull becomes a bullet out of a barrel—a projectile—and the horses, technologies, and men the rocket launcher. Heat-seeking, dangerous, partially predictable, the bull is still umbilically connected to the original assembly, a mere agent of the gun. Freedom is short. He is soon back in the cradle of horses and men. Transformation is the mode of operation, linear and continuous, replication and morphing. A form of humid rhetoric in which life and technology produce transformers along axes of condensation (all components become one) and displacement (stirrups lose importance when the bull is free). The key here is the *line of flight*—the enormous power projected by the bull's desire to run free, to abandon his bondage and to transform it into freedom. This power is the Ariadne's thread that leads back and out of the pen, in and out of the Feria. If there is a bull's logic, it is trajectorial and ballistic. It seeks freedom, and if necessary combat, all fueled by reproductive heat commingled with the freedom of the range.

The rider's will, the bull's desire, and various automatic processes such as the running characteristics of bulls and horses (Muybridge) point at the complex interaction between the automatic and the willed. There is a startling beauty in this synthesis of the given and the designed that reflects on our future relationship to the logic of a more narrow design machine, the computer. The automatic becomes labor-saving, time out, time-to-think-time, in which the next willed interference may be planned. (Even the circadian rhythm has been changed here, when young designers building complex models go to sleep when the machine renders, regardless of night or day.) The automatic is here to stay, but like the bull it has to be reined in occasionally.

The design machine projected here is of the first generation. The closeness between components reflects this primacy. Friction and force make up a (finally catastrophic) set of very close relations. The ergonomic demands are greater and more necessary than any philosophical or aesthetic demands. There are much tighter fits needed between the salient parts of the bull/men/horse/machine than the bull pen. This suggests a spectrum, characterized by extreme closeness at one end (the machine at hand) and vague ephemeral relations at the other, such as in a public plaza.

■

The refocusing on machinic assemblages of the wet kind is a reflection of the loss of hold of the purely symbolic over many of us. Form and figure are no longer forced but found in the materials at hand: the bull's displacement, his speed, the horses' strength, the capability of the riders to shape and deform that strength. Emancipated from the ideology of sign systems—of wished-for meaning—the modern designer can no longer shape his or her material from without, leaving the matter of construction to the technicians. Designers must become the design opportunity, join force with the bull's line of flight, with domestic cycles and economies in the design of a house, of a widget for stirring a pot, or in the layout of an assembly of houses. For better or worse we have left to market forces the minor questions of why, and we may now concentrate on how to do it. (Major *why* questions still remain in the political realm, and here the belief in the embryo of goodness in all people may be the only hope for a common morality.)

The bias of the new design machine is form, formation, and use not in stasis but in motion, as much process as product: the *rush* of design and use rather than the rest. The racing thought as the built: the *map*—the lines, fluxes, and emissions (Deleuze)—as well as figures and forms. Invariably each assembly begins with "fuel," tools, and a context of disparate things, people, and circumstances that are then brought together in "proximity groupings," ranging from near to far. One may suggest, slyly, obliquely, that in such proximity groupings not only the designer but the user or dweller are implicated. The customary tight net thrown around form alone is completely discredited, because of its lack of depth and its narrow horizon. Consequently in the new design machine we must explore simultaneously the depth of the materials involved and the sphere of insinuation that surrounds each design proposition. Physics, chemistry, and propensity on the one hand and sociology, psychology, economics, politics, and desire on the other—points and lines (depth and surface). Although certain characteristics of this new machine may remind us of functionalism, it is not a neofunctionalism but rather a type of *vitalism* that comes to mind. Vitalism in the sense of trying to capture the inherent characteristics and movements of both material and dweller. A gathering of (life) forces rather than the subjugation of material for the benefit of use. The way to such machinery is long and tortuous because we know so little about ourselves and our materials. The bull machine, seemingly simple and inevitable, surely took long to develop. Trial and error, reaching deeper and deeper into bull's, horses' and men's psyches and wider and wider into the city and its rituals. The new design machine must take the long perspective too, despite the increasing demand for speed.

Household Vehicles

In 1968, a bookcase shaped by the widths of books rather than their average heights began the project for suburban furniture. In retrospect, this inauspicious beginning is of importance because of its assault on a convention. Like levers on a great unwieldy machine, the subsequent Household Vehicles have served as buildings may do for experimental architects, or as experiments for scientists. Furniture stands at the threshold between dweller and dwelling (in both of its meanings), where the body meets the world. My furniture has a genealogy. Running in parallel with conventional architecture projects, the furniture seems often more relevant to my inquiry: a curiosity about the relationships between architecture as the fixed, furniture as the movable (as in French *meuble*), and the dweller as the agent of action. And in particular, my curiosity and unease about the cartoonish fixity of the dynamic aspects of the same equation in suburbia. Once inscribed on the other, or read through, the vehicles, their imagined agents, and the settings become tests of thought experiments, the tokens of my preoccupation with daily life in the metropolis.

In 1987, a chair is the site of the fusion of low and high culture. The fusion of an Adirondack chair and Rietveld's Red and Blue chair is an exercise in rhetorical transformation (rotation, displacement, ellipsis), and a built trace of the migration from the front porch to the TV room, at the introduction of the air conditioner. Fusion, rhetorical transformations, and change, central subjects of my curiosity.

Looking out through the *fenêtre en longueur* while ascending the ramp in a Corbusian villa, the new man is inadvertently about to exhaust the sectional technologies, if not his body. Moving in the footsteps of the architect's homunculus, he has been slowly rotated in space to get the full effect: technology in the service of the architect's point of view. And when the new man reaches the *toit-jardin*, the panoramic view is of an idealized city.

The corresponding view from Ray and Charles Eames's glass wall in their house in a Los Angeles canyon is atomized, dispersed, and obscured by a kaleidoscope of images. Here the city has disappeared. Panoramic vision and transformational technologies have been displaced by a distribution of images, gifts to the senses. And the chair that you sit in is form-fitted, while an equally shapely leg splint is cradling your broken leg, gently holding you forth to the ocular feast.

The Household Vehicles, critically inspired and affected by these visions, attempt to move closer and further away simultaneously. The pragmatics of Corbu's sectional technologies, the intersubjective compassion of Eames chair and leg splint, combined with skepticism, conjure up images of personal technologies that hint, serve, submit, and question. Panorama, introspection, and doubt at the same time.

After the tapered bookcase and the fused chair, new vehicles were designed in 1989 for a Plan Degree Zero. The which-way-mirror, in which two inhabitants face each other across the mirror, makes them "share" each other's legs or torso. The sofa/bed begs the user's choice. The which-way-chair makes a pair of dwellers point in opposite directions while still seeing each other. The Last Supper table is her way of saying: this is the last time. Gathered together in a complex sentence, these domestic devices are separated from the fixed architectural setting. Transformers, vehicles of interaction, community devices, machines for intersubjectivity, versatility, and choice (fig. 43). This separation is a step in the genealogy. In the Nofamily House of 1983 architecture's fixity is assaulted by a series of traps that unsettles the use and meaning of architectural components: handrails, windows, doors, stairs, and walls. Again the dweller must choose.

These assemblies of dualities, drawn only, to accompany projects for houses, establish a neutrality. A plan where all Corbusian directionality, or Eamesian comfort, is arrested or delayed. Built narratives are held back, waiting for the dweller. The suburban house plan, like all intentional arrangements of domestic space, is implicated and put into question: is a room (assigned by its location in the plan as a living room) a living room when occupied by a sofa that is simultaneously a bed? Or is the room a bedroom? The answer is not in the plan but the dweller's. Freedom at last!

These *planned assaults* on domestic arrangement led in 1990–1998 to a new series of household vehicles. Under the influence of Samuel Beckett's second novel *Watt*, they were designed and built as part of a museum installation called *room* (figs. 33–41).

In *Watt*, Watt and Knott, manservant and master, play out a seemingly absurd pantomime. The two, Watt's reflections, his emotions, and Knott's paraphernalia lay out an entire map of imaginable everyday actions. This map serves as the Ariadne's thread for the Household Vehicles. Unencumbered by a surrounding, played out in a large house, although still lodged in English class society, Watt's world is strangely suburban, and so are his thoughts.

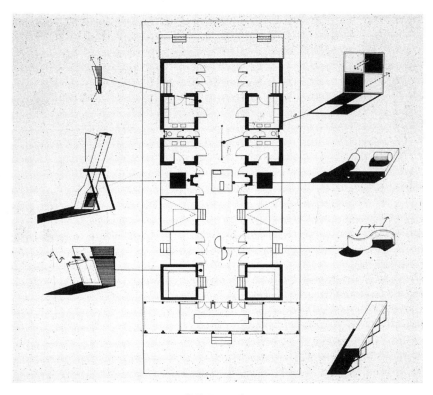

43 *First generation*

Watt did not know whether he was glad or sorry that he didn't see Mr. Knott more often. In one sense he was sorry, and in another glad. And the sense in which he was sorry was this, that he wished to see Mr. Knott face to face, and the sense in which he was glad was this, that he feared to do so. Yes indeed, in so far as he wished, in so far as he feared, to see Mr. Knott face to face, his wish made him sorry, his fear glad, that he saw him so seldom, and at such a great distance as a rule, and so fugitively, and so often sideways on, and often even from behind.[48]

In the gentle absurdity of Watt's sorrow and gladness lies for me the suburban formlessness "unstable, precarious, transitory": the ethos of the protean field.

Lives being played out in this field are gently tugged at by mild fears, intangible pressures, and held in place while driven by routines and structural limitations. Stepping out of the house, your neighbor is exactly a house lot away, and you cannot see if he has shaved or if she wears makeup and the house itself is caught in a freeze frame. A million loci held in place by freeways, cul-de-sacs, and invisible mortgage institutions. Despite a steady change of hands, and the speed and vigor of the protean field they sit in, these loci do not move an inch. The house, although lacking the upstairs-downstairs of Mr. Knott's, still plays out its compartmentalizations. Now horizontally, in built form and human behavior, regardless of the personality and character of its inhabitants, following the same grammar: living, dining, kitchen, garage (and lately more garage), family room, TV room, and den. The actions, when laid out, exposed, and reflected upon, are shockingly close to Watt's and Knott's map:

> This room was furnished solidly and with taste.
>
> This solid and tasteful furniture was subjected by Mr. Knott to frequent changes of position, both absolute and relative. Thus it was not rare to find, on the Sunday, the tallboy on its feet by the fire, and the dressing-table on its head by the bed, and the night-stool on its face by the door, and the wash-hand-stand on its back by the window; and, on the Monday, the tallboy on its back by the bed, and the dressing-table on its face by the door, and the night-stool on its back by the window, and the wash-hand-stand on its feet by the fire; and, on the Tuesday, the tallboy on its face by the door, and the dressing-table on its back by the window, and the night-stool on its feet by the fire, and the wash-hand-stand on its head by the bed; and, on the Wednesday, the tallboy on its back by the window, and the dressing-table on its feet by the fire, and the night-stool on its head by the bed, and the wash-hand-stand on its face by the door; and, on the Thursday, the tallboy on its side by the fire, and the dressing-table on its feet by the bed, and the night-stool on its head by the door, and the wash-hand-stand on its face by the window; and, on the Friday, the tallboy on its feet by the bed, and the dressing-table on its head by the door, and the night-stool on its face the window, and the wash-hand-stand on its side by the fire; and . . .[49]

Suburban life as pantomime of overly repeated behaviors is, when accumulated over time and territory, absurd too; or better, Watt and Knott are not.

Energetically Corbu's new man runs up the stairs to the *toit-jardin*—the end of the architectural promenade—only to slump down in the gentle prosthetic hold of an Eames chair, when he realizes that beyond the view there is no there there. The demise of the utopian promise. At the moment of this reflection, all his accumulated actions are dauntingly meaningless. It may be at precisely this moment of hesitation, of incomprehensibility, of the meaningless, that the Household Vehicles roll in:

> The automaton [as first-order simulacra] plays the part of the courtier and good company; it participates in the pre-Revolutionary French theatrical and social games. The robot, on the other hand, as his name indicates, is a worker: the theater is over and done with, the reign of mechanical man commences.[50]

The array of traps and vehicles strives to delay the everyday narrative, to amuse to be sure, to divert yes, but more important to help free the dweller from the stereotypical, the prescribed, the expected. The Tallboy brings the traditional tripartite English storage unit on four legs forward by outfitting it with wheels and assigning it to the storage of books. Simultaneously with this transformation, an array of *differentiated* references are *integrated*: the wheelbarrow, the library ladder, the Roman war machine, the cheese grater, St. Sebastian's sagittation, the attack on the book. As memory banks, the automatons begin to write complex sets of interconnected yet incomplete narratives while engaging the dweller's body. The engagement demanded by the tripartite household vehicle named O'Meldon's Cube and Root compels characters from *Watt*: Mr. MacStern to open, Louit to look, Mr. Nackybal to kick open, and Mr. Fitzwein to insert. "An episode in the *Kulturkampf*, said Mr. O'Meldon"[51] fortuitously, since it points at the very crux of the problem with the suburban house: its mind-numbing fixity, and how in a microscopic way we can begin the assault and its eventual undoing. Culture wars indeed.

> It was not long before I saw, in the other fence, another hole, in the position opposite, and similar in shape, to that through which, some ten of fifteen minutes before, I had made my way. . . . For if the two holes had

been independently burst, the one from Watt's side of Watt's fence, and the other from mine of mine, by two quite different infuriated boars, or bulls . . . then their conjunction, at this point, was incomprehensible, to say the least.[52]

The dweller stands contrary to architecture, as the soft body in face of a hard wall. Yet architecture is mind's body. It is through the apertures of these two bodies that the Household Vehicles attempt to burst. A gentle and playful bursting to be sure; distraction is more likely than transcendence. But then there is no way of knowing, when it comes to people and their machines.

Toward Fusion

Fusion as an existential question may always have been present in my work, hammering at the doors of various autonomies. Fusion is present in the union of the Adirondack and Rietveld chairs, between dwellers and their furniture in the Household Vehicles, between functions in the suburban plan leading to a Plan Degree Zero, and between nature and culture. In Villa Prima Facie of 1975, the first embryonic steps are taken toward the fusion of the latter (fig. 27).

Architecturally, a paradigmatic shift from architects' common obsession with the plan to the material of the walls is brought to the fore by keeping the distance between each wall the same (and therefore making each room identical) and concentrating attention on the "baroque" walls. The emphasis on materiality brings us to nature: the dry sand of the desert, the hot flume of the volcano, the brittle surface of ice, the bubbling wetness of a waterfall. Each wall, materialized, produces different spheres of insinuation that bring (colluding) dwellers away and out from their habitual doings. The walls at Prima Facie are not about the science of materials but closer to a psychology of materials, fueled by Gaston Bachelard's obsession with fire.

The final enclosing of the array of walls in a greenhouse suggests that a botanical propensity may be present. The step toward "growing the house" is not far away. At the outset of the house a soft topiary wall forms the entry. Placed just outside the forcing house, watered automatically by the runoff from its roof, the soft wall opens naively toward things to come, while dwellers have to use their shears to keep its shape.

■

In light of the insinuating presence of nature, a suburban design machine demands the explorations of material, its physics and chemistry. But it is unlikely that at the synthetic moment, when all the forces of nature and culture are brought together, the *Ineinsbildung* (the into-one-making or esemplastic) will be a simple fusion between the behavior and science of a set of materials. Instead the designer must find the *propensity* of the material, a concept borrowed rather frivolously in light of its distinguished history in Chinese thinking.[53] This *vitality* is both given and willed. Not totally automatic, the propensity in the new design machine is an unacknowledged promiscuity, in which the designer merges with the material. Like swimmers in the summer-warm Rhine in Basel, the designer goes downstream immersed in the material, finding its inclination and making use of it to design, a give and take. Clearly, media constraints have always existed, but all too often the material has been seen as an adversary, urging the designer to use force and mastery rather than an amalgam of will and complicity. The next iteration of the fusion of material and technology requires (for me) a major paradigmatic shift in which the physics and chemistry of material and, alas, its propensity are the focus. The step to what Louis Kahn called the *will* of the material is long and cumbersome, since any kind of inherent science of propensity is deeply embedded and therefore utterly incomprehensible without extensive scientific and practical experimentation.

The character of the division between nature and artificiality has come to recent public attention. The bioengineering of the common potato has erased for good what is left of the division. We are again facing serious ethical and existential questions, although further development is inevitable, as are future disasters. However, even in a market-driven economy where "abuse of material" (in apparent favor of process and cost) is commonplace, discoveries in tune with the material will not only result in lowered costs and increased efficiency but in positive environmental and cultural effects. The positive results will be more likely when and if our methods of transforming nature become more sophisticated, which always means *simpler* (often contrary to the complex science necessary for understanding), leading to an engineering of materials as energy-conserving as nature—the emergence of biomimetics.

The Simple House

The first day of summer. The motorboat is jammed with groceries, clothes, sails, fishing gear, tools, books, and anticipation. The wind is still cold. Eyes watering, we steer out of the harbor—out on the first open flat of water—in between the two first navigation beacons, red and green. Trying to reconnect our sea legs, we sway and stumble while the vigorous sea heaves. The roar of the outboard motor drowns all conversation and we are left to our own reveries.

The sea we are entering is the Baltic, the city we are leaving behind is Stockholm, and its archipelago, purportedly fifty-two thousand islands, lies ahead. But this is no virgin voyage. Thousands of others will do the same, because in the course of the three summer months, in shifts, we all go on *semester*. Semester, or vacation, is the prize for our labors. The endless light is our redemption. The galaxy's splendid gift.

This habit of leaving the city for a painfully short yet exhilarating encounter with nature is also a reliving of the lives of our ancestors, although theirs were mostly hard labor when as farmers they changed gear to harvest a momentary abundance of herring. Tracing these voyages from land to sea and back is for the moderns a ritual of renewal, shedding the complexities and worries of the city, shedding work for rest, replacing everyday life with the simple life of the islands. Should work disappear, its last memories would reappear here when, slowly, boats leave the city behind and head into the wind.

The voyage between city and island, work and *semester*, is emblematic of all commutes. A ritual performed by millions, every day, all across the terrapolis. Seen in this light, the daily commute, performed by Swedish-Americans driving to work in St. Paul, Minnesota, as well as their relatives taking the subway to work in Stockholm, takes on an epic dimension. The thirty-four man-years spent commuting, every day, in metropolitan Houston is not just the result of a technological shift from the horse to the car, but our destiny. A destiny that is our nomadic past: our restlessness, our predilection to escape, to run away, our savage heart. In Stockholm this yearly ritual is particularly graphic because so public, so predictable: the summer hats, the sandals (and the ankle socks), the cameras, and the endless plastic bags crowding the aisles on the subways, in buses, in commuter trains, and on ferries. The huffing and the puffing, the slight irritation, and the anticipation, writ large below sweaty brows.

Yet the tradition is simplicity. On the islands (here serving as a metaphor for the holes in the holey plane) there is rarely running water, no sewerage or septic tanks, no cars, since human occupation is so short and the islands so small and so disconnected from the infrastructures of the city. Surrounding *kobbarna och skaren* (the islands), modernity in the shape of boats, rowed, sailed, motorized, and combinations thereof, slow or fast, well-sailed or aggressively pushed for peak performance, large and small, crisscross the waters, reminding us that the city is not too far away, particularly in mind and attitude. Yet even the ear-shattering noise of a polluting two-stroke engine fades, once the first autumn storm signals the return of nature's rule. The cyclical occupation allows the islands the necessary respite to replenish rainwater cisterns, to return human waste to soil, to let the microbiological processes reform the pollutants, and to replace the drinking songs with nature's own ambiguous moans.

The islands now surrounding us, alternatively forming narrow sounds or more distant large flats of water, were "constructed" by the receding inland ice that, some eight thousand years ago, slowly retreated, in its wake carving out valleys and ridges, fingers spread, a giant hand on a sand beach. Some of these clusters of valleys and ridges formed islands, others remained under water, shaping the habitat for fish and algae.

Cutting across the last expanse of water, almost due east, *vita gass*—"white geese"—spray us with mists of brackish water, while our island bulks up on the horizon. Landing, as is our custom, we bump the pier hard, as if to kick off the summer and close a year of work. In the plastic hull at the bow, we add a fresh dent to two others. This way we keep count. Our island has forty other families, no cars, no roads, no stores, but electricity, paths, and some deep wells with gloriously clean drinking water. On this island the striations run north-south, the most common direction since the ice generally went north. The soil is thin and gathered in the valleys. A large central valley with rich soil supported a farmer-fisher family during the early part of the twentieth century. Now an abundant kitchen garden supplies us with strawberries, new potatoes, raspberries, salad, and carrots. However, rock rather than soil is ground zero. The natural vegetation is tough and resilient: mostly conifers, with some birch, oak, and beech. The valleys are (in season) covered with berries and wild grasses. The spring flowers last until the end of July. Hunters and gatherers have lived here since the end of the Ice Age. The aristocracy and later the middle class have inhabited the islands, mostly during the summer and only in the nineteenth and twentieth centuries.

We reach the house by climbing (and carrying and, at the cusp, dragging our luggage) some sixty feet above the water. A stunning panorama of islands and open water fills the view to the horizon. Cumulonimbus stack fake, white islands above us as if mirroring the true islands below. But they are gray and heavy, as if the granite—defying gravity—is about to rain. We sway from the ride and our heads spin. The blue water and sky fade seamlessly into each other. Summer has begun.

Our house is a cabin, simple, built predominantly of wood, placed directly on the granite rock. Essentially prefabricated, it was built around 1965 by three carpenters. No running water or sewage. The design is a distillation of Swedish functionalism: living room-kitchen-dining, two small sleeping cabins, and some storage. A trickle-down design from the great functionalist era of Asplund and Lewerentz. A building designer working for the fabricator designed our house. The veranda, the living room with its picture windows, and the dining area face the grand view in which the islands in the panorama are layered to form a natural theater in which the only variants are boats, birds, and weather. Carefully maintained, the house seems unfazed by thirty years of battering by use, weather, and wind.

At first we had ambitions to add and change, but with the realization that everything that is added (or subtracted) has to be carried up (or down) the sixty feet across very rough terrain, we came to look at changes with a minimalist eye. Conservation of energy, mostly my energy (only once did I buy beer in glass bottles). It occurred to us that *tinkering and modification* (instead of starting from a tabula rasa) are in themselves a design strategy that is effectively used by people of limited power but with some measure of ingenuity. Lévi-Strauss the French anthropologist talked about the great resourcefulness of the *bricoleur*, the jack-of-all-trades who makes use of the discarded by reassembling and inventing new uses for old things. Consequently we have come to think of our house, the old furniture left within, the tools, even the pictures on the walls as nature, as givens, as potential *readymades*. All we have to do is to hone and tweak them. The desire to make all of it ours is strong, so the task is to bring all these givens across the line to the taken. The readymade was an invention of Marcel Duchamp, one of the most influential artist-thinkers of the twentieth century. Notoriously he presented a urinal, rotated on its back, as a fountain in an exhibition in New York. Despite the public's shock, Duchamp showed that by simply changing the context of an object—by changing its grammar—it would acquire new significance. In a more general sense all the consumer objects that litter our daily lives are potential readymades, just waiting for the turn, the misuse, the misplacement.

Our new view of the house and its environs had a profound effect on our attitude. All of this happened very fast, so fast that we sensed a geological shift in which the givens that we had liked or disliked all became valuable and likable, in need only of tweaking. Even the ugly fake-peasant furniture of the sixties became a potential asset that could be rushed across the line into what we consider artful. Looking back over this shift, I realize that architecture has moved out of the center and that the field of application is now much wider, including a whole array of concerns ranging from the gathering and preparation of mushrooms to building—all under the general rubric of *making*. Architecture, design, cooking, and art have been replaced by the more generic making. Generalized making in unison with thinking form a strategy for an existence, albeit a privileged one, but one driven by an openness rather than by a narrow discriminating view in which few if any objects and actions pass muster. Architects with their carefully honed aesthetic concerns fail here, since they live and die to create a world according to their own narrow ideology. This narrowness is in my view debilitating, because it forecloses so many options. However, the alternative strategy presented here does not lack ideology or an aesthetic position. But since it is compromised by the given, or rather since it never starts from scratch but always with the given, the result is always a reflection of the given and the taken. When I carve hangers from juniper, the characteristic bow in its branches will always permeate my attempts to seek my own shapes. The bow, the result of a built-in feedback mechanism present in all branches, juts out from the trunk only to turn vertical after an inch or two. These characteristic bends and verticals add up to the overall lozenge shape of the tree, while allowing the greenery its necessary *Lebensraum*. The bends make the juniper distinct and different from other conifers where the stems of each branch jut out straight from the trunk. Trees when observed this closely reveal an uncanny "intelligence" in which shape and feedback mechanisms play an important role. My hangers, fastened to the walls of the house, illustrate the characteristic bend of the juniper better than the tree, since the greenery has been removed. The conceptual distance is vast between the juniper branch (and its relations to the host trunk) and the typical two-by-four milled to serve the construction of the house.

Although there is a strong desire to come closer to the wisdom of the aboriginal forest, the current work on the island is at this point but a step closer to the energy-conserving position of nature. (An attempt on my part, like a crab, to move sideways into ecology without stumbling into its fascist inclinations.) The intervention—the turning of an everyday object into a new object, a builder's house into architecture, a branch into a hanger, or chanterelles into *pasta ai funghi*—require both *fortuna* and *virtù*, both luck and skill. The fake-peasant chairs are a case in point. It took a considerable time of reflection before I brought out the dull handsaw and decapitated the chair. Most of the decoration and the handle were removed, making the chair less functional, the cut crude. But it looks almost right, particularly once painted battleship gray. The old and the new are always visible in the juxtaposition between the old smooth, carefully tooled chair and the new fast, rough, and abrasive intervention. The stained horizontal siding on the house is next.

The veranda table needs work. The glossy white coat does not work. Tilting, it sits on a drop cloth on the sloping rock that is our front yard. For a second the table mirrors the cumulus clouds that race above us, while seen against the black islands resting in the watery theater beyond. Mimesis and fusion! Black islands in the shape of clouds gather on the table. The paint, the brush, and the hand bridge the sky and sea. From today we will eat on what is above and below us. Emerson wrote correspondingly, "The whirling bubble on the surface of a brook, admits us to the secret of the mechanics of the sky."[54]

Lights and the newly installed water are turned off. Our boat is already in the marina waiting for its turn to take its winter rest under a green tarpaulin. While we turn to look, risking a spill on the steep rock path, the simple house has returned to its Cinderella sleep. The ferry takes us back. Surreptitiously rest slips into work.

■

Architecture, design, architect, designer, reconsidered are components of a Pandora's box with no clear limits. The designer in the suburban metropolis must turn toward distributed design, leaving in its wake the ancient barricades around architectural autonomy while opening the gates toward nature and the propensity of things. The erasure of the distinction between subject and object in the design machine signals the end of the binary and opens the gate to the design not only of things but of humans. Le Corbusier's new man will appear a simpleton next to the redesigned humans of the future.

IV
The
Frontier

Buoyed by expectation, maybe fortified by discovery, yet bewildered by the opaque panorama, we are back in the suburban metropolis. Still seeking, but now for a frontier where we can play out a distributed architecture and situate its architects. Searching the suburban metropolis for its frontier is confusing. In a country where going west still claims its enthusiasts, one might assume that the edge of growth is the frontier. But looking closely at the utterly predictable cookie-cutter expansions, often on former farmland, instantly kills any hopes of finding the frontier. Anything less inspiring and more predictable is hard to imagine. And talking to Edge City developers is further confirmation, since predictability is precisely what they want and ostensibly what they get. Compass and growth are no longer good predictors. We must search elsewhere.

The Middle Landscape

The stretch of urbanity between Downtown and the suburban en-
claves—the Holey Plane—is motionless in the dense summer heat. The
large swaths of empty space, regularly interspersed with the built, are
teeming with nature, mosquitoes, fire ants, and, under the trees, shade
for the weary. The black parking pools of asphalt—the Strands of Hell—
boil. The incessant hum of air conditioners and their persistent drip set
this scene of unglamorous construction to a beat. Yet in its eclectic mish-
mash, in its foregrounding of urban process over form (even over the grid
since it is often broken), the Plane teems with restless anticipation.

Frontiers

The frontier is a heterogeneous subject, especially since it is increasingly mythical if
not already fictional. Its recent shorthand history is tragic. After the Second World
War the frontier turned introspective, and under the auspices of urban renewal the
inner city became the new frontier. The medico-military model, probably nurtured
during the Great War, replaced the unregulated energy driving earlier frontiers, but
with very dubious results. With the end of the Vietnam War, the *Mash* spirit seeking
to heal urban sickness with radical surgery, hardware, and military strategy has lost
its credibility. Very recently, after decades of inaction, a new, most unlikely frontier
force has arisen: the Nimbys (Not In My Back Yard), now reaching a logical conclusion in the BANANAs (Build Absolutely Nothing Anywhere Near Anyone)—an effete
type of citizen-guerillas that form momentary coalitions to stop a projected development. Vietnam still haunts the nation in more than one way, while its most recent
frontier has become a Norman Rockwell painting holding onto a utopia of the past.

The relationships between frontiers and the new metropolis are synthetic and in-
scrutable. The vast metropolitan surface is greatly uneven, harboring only fragments of the various frontiers, more or less calcified. To begin to search this surface
for the most vibrant frontier, we must turn to the new metropolitan vocabulary: to
megashapes and to their internal characteristics, their ecology.

If still permeated by the promise of opportunity, the new frontier must belong to
those who continue to suffer the city. "A clearing in the woods was infinitely prefer-

able to unemployment in a city street," wrote Philip Guedalla about those who experienced the economic slump of 1837. Despite the persistent but now faint glow of the west, we must look closer to the suffering for the "clearing" in the frontier ecology. In reference to the city, Reyner Banham, in his book on Los Angeles, used the concept of ecologies.[1] He never defined what he meant by an ecology, but it is evident that he thought the common arsenal of concepts, such as district or neighborhood, was inadequate in describing the complexity and specificity of the relationships between dwellers and their settings in a city. Since ecology is undiscriminating in its recognition of relationships, it seems a particularly apt concept in a metropolis where city form is equal to time, location, geography, and weather. Banham wanted to capture not just the physical aspect of Surfurbia or the Planes of Id, but the atmosphere, the smell, the pulse (or lack thereof), and the spirit as well as the landscape, the infrastructure, and the buildings. He understood that the narrow definitions of architects and planners failed to include what we today call *software*. (Among the many revolutions of the computer, the concept of software has helped us understand that a world is not completely described by an operating system.) It is safe to surmise from Banham's analysis that most metropolitan regions consist of a series of very specific subecologies. However, it is also safe to postulate that there are within the same regions, among different conurbations, ecologies that, although specific and unique in some respects, also share common characteristics that make it possible to develop a more generic classification. It is safe to say that most metropolitan areas have downtowns (or remnants or facsimiles thereof) and a variety of centers that can be described in ecological terms. When visually coherent, some of these ecologies are also megashapes. It is also evident that in some stages of the evolution of downtown it was seen as a frontier. This is no longer the case, since we will find formerly proud high-rise buildings prostrate in suburban office parks—genuflecting as it were to capital (and more predictable labor markets), hardly the image of the frontier.

However, there is another generic ecology, common in all suburban metropolises, known enigmatically since Leo Marx as the middle landscape. This ecology applies to large domains in Houston, Dallas, Phoenix, Los Angeles, Orlando, Atlanta, the Ruhrgebiet, and even in the German extension of such quaint cities as Basel, Switzerland. Located between defined domains (downtown and suburb), the middle landscape is unfinished, incomplete, waiting somewhere between development and squalor. Hard to grasp, hard to write, even in its most rational and technical aspects, this territory is an in-between, neither here nor there. This landscape in the middle has its history, its depth and breadth, and ubiquitousness, which even in the example of Houston, in the face of its relative youth, is all but two-dimensional. Houston's middle landscape dominates large areas of the inner loop. Unlike Downtown, the Medical Center, or the Galleria, the middle landscape remains baffling, even at closer scrutiny. And in this enigma lies the frontier spirit.

In discussing the city, Michel de Certeau identified the "imbricated strata"—the palimpsest of habits, practices, physical traces, accretions and subtractions and overlays of memories—as a fertility, the controverted growing ground of urban culture. Benjamin in his *Berliner Chronik* wrote, "remembrance . . . must, in the strictest and rhapsodic manner, assay its spade in ever-new places . . . and ever deeper"[2] strata. Applied to Houston's middle landscape, these two observations reveal a stuttering, indeterminate, and incomplete *middlescape* (half city, half nature) spreading like a paste with wildly varying thickness across the plain, dotted by oaks and other luxuriant greenery. An almost intact grid of streets organizes the middlescape into a technocratic ledger open to speculation. Yet opposing forces, paths, and habits counteract a too simplistic interpretation. As de Certeau writes:

> However, beneath the fabrication and universal writing of technology opaque and stubborn places remain. The revolutions of history, economic mutations, demographic mixtures lie in layers within it, and remain there, hidden in customs, rites and spatial practices. The legible discourses that formerly articulated them have disappeared, or left only fragments in language. This place, on its surface, seems to be a collage. In reality, in its depth it is ubiquitous. A piling of heterogeneous places. Each one, like a deteriorating page in a book, refers to a different mode of territorial unity, of socioeconomic distribution, of political conflicts and of identifying symbolism.[3]

Although an image of utter tranquillity, particularly in days of little new construction, the middle landscape is deceptively homogeneous. This deception is partially maintained because of our own blindness, but most important because of the "subtle and compensatory equilibria that silently guarantee complementariness."[4]

It is as if everything, despite its profound and deep difference, is painted, if not in the same color, at least in the same hue. Generous, forgiving, forgetful, this plane divulges none of its secrets too easily.

Highly uneven, sometimes articulate, occasionally in the making, there is much to read in the middle landscape, particularly when distinguished by type and function: a new medical museum, a Holocaust memorial, a refurbished housing project consisting of three apartment U's, a horse riding stable, and swatches of still virgin land. Yet this legibility is just the reflection of the rational techniques that still dominate the architecture and planning profession. The three U's were just last year the severely deteriorated apartment block for two dozen families or fragments thereof. Their lives have been erased—their recent crude removal being a most graphic expression: this *erasure* has been long in the making. After all, some families harbor three generations of unemployment. Standing above them as I did for two years, I saw these people silhouetted against the rules and regulations manifested in their *Existenzminimum* apartments eking out a meager existence. We can only hope that their tactics of survival (de Certeau), against most odds, had a measure of success despite the frequent violence, the occasional fire, the police raid, and daily sweet seductions of *Señor Azúcar*—the Good Humor man. Next door the public park, the museums, and the stable allow the children of these beleaguered families to encounter *the open city*. Here the facilities of the metropolis, open and accessible, have not yet closed down the full thermodynamics of the old city. Yet just beyond the trees, on the outside of the loop, the grid that assumes access to all is frequently broken to allow for the few and privileged to live out their paranoias. Whole hives of enclaves are subdividing the city.

The enigma of the middle landscape is not without its contours, outlines, and shapes. Some are more readable than others, and some more purposeful. The Museum District is such a formation, although it is evident that the very nature of the middle landscape—its stuttering, its hesitancies, its gaps—have impinged here too.[5]

Museum Geography

At first it is only the road signs; then, after several street crossings, the district itself emerges, or rather the museum buildings; and only then the district begins to come forth, if not take shape. The Museum District is not a Berlin *Museum Insel*, with a distinct urban shape or location, but more an atmosphere (vapor) with subtle reminders about its presence: slightly higher densities, occasional large buildings, some semipublic space, and Modern Architecture, but no perspectival presentation, no network of boulevards, no civic conclusions, no public plazas. Not yet a megashape, the district is a *grain*, offering a certain level of discrete pattern recognition. Located between the Medical Center and Downtown, it has no precise borders. As in sprawl, the seekers have to do some work to find their prey. Once they find it, there is always parking.

The Menil Collection is both the subtlest and the most powerful demonstration of this peculiarly suburban commitment to public life. Neatly arranged on nine blocks right in the middle of the *Mittellandschaft*, the Collection is discovered almost by accident, even once the visitor sort-of-knows where it is. Frustrating? Maybe, but suburban!—the gentle reminder of our itinerant inclinations.

The buildings belonging to the Menil Foundation are an almost picture-perfect demonstration of Jefferson's University of Virginia,[6] complete with a subtle critique of any mercantile tendencies.[7] The museum, designed by Renzo Piano, the Italian architect, during the early 1980s and inaugurated in 1987, is a simple box housing some hidden complexities: sophisticated technologies, a museum and curatorial program. The building displaced a series of bungalows, some of which were inserted in the surrounding blocks, also owned by the foundation. The "lawn" on which the museum sits at one end reaches over four blocks, the Rothko Chapel occupying the other end. The Jeffersonian rotunda as museum box has been displaced and has lost some of its symbolic prominence, to find a more ambivalent and suburban position. There is a front entrance reached by a lawn, but there is also a fairly prominent back entrance. The public can enter both. The back acts almost like a city building, making a perimeter with the sidewalk. A loggia surrounding the building adds an "agrarian urbanity" bringing Jefferson's university back in focus. However, Piano's pavilions are not attached to the loggia but simply inserted in their proper slots, following the regimented principles of the typical blocks surrounding the museum. And we would not know that they were Jeffersonian pavilions if they were not all painted gray, just like the museum itself. In a powerful display of rhetorical skill, the gray has replaced the physical value of the loggia with the visual value of a common color.[8] This type of transfiguration and transformation of a principle, deliberate or not (as is most certainly the case here), is evidence that the foundation understood something profound about the middle landscape it was about to grace with its presence.

Piano's museum is a situational tour de force. The much-discussed *leaves* form an artificial canopy that systematically and selectively opens the sky to the galleries, mimicking the leaves of the zoohemic canopy: an exemplary demonstration of how architecture can write itself into a specific ecology, if not yet with trees' photosynthetic capabilities. Critics' quibbles with the leaves, their material and expensive technology, have been predictably pedantic and fail to recognize that the conceptual quality—their message—is far more important than how it was worked out. In turn, the Twombly Gallery (in the shape of a pavilion properly situated on the adjacent block in a mix of small institutions and dwellings) is zoohemic, outfitted with a second-generation canopy, confirming Piano's commitment to working on the ecology.

Nestled in the outer reaches of the loose yarn of the Museum District, the Menil properties meet the surrounding urban tissue shamelessly, creating, in contradistinction to the common suburban encirclements, a *soft enclave*. A thickening of urban form and plot: more and diverse shapes and stims, all suspended in the middle landscape. Like a case study project, the Menil Collection demonstrates one productive direction for the evolution of the Museum District. Although all the museums have made attempts to expand their public apron, the lack of space and jurisdiction has stalled any effort to make further connections. And this is fortuitous, because that may not be the genetic inclination of the middle landscape.

Looking over the Museum District (and from the 28th floor I can see glimpses of six of the seven major museums), one is struck by the internal coherence of each museum and the external formlessness of the district. The total lack of physical (or stylistic) similarity between museums, aside from sharing a common district, is typical of the multicentered metropolis. In addition, classical and late modernist planning would suggest that all the museums be physically connected. Yet, looking closer, one sees that each museum contains functional similarities: often an increasingly similar weight is laid on the museum shop and the galleries (aside from the Menil, which remains stoically noncommercial). Having seen one museum, the drifter navigating the district will not be surprised by the next museum, although he or she may be surprised by the radical difference in design quality.[9]

What if the museums decided to cooperate, what should they do? Build a network of boulevards and plazas? A new sign system, or a navigating device, such as a Hand Pilot? How should they attempt to fictionalize the experience[10] of going to the museum, of being within the vapors of urban culture?

Although the open museum (Malraux) has been a concern among museologists, it has invariably meant a concern with the museum's interior and its relation to an audience. In the city, museums found their logical places in the hierarchy of public infrastructure. Openness to the city was not an issue. In Houston's Museum District little such order exists, and yet this disorder is the key to its openness.

In Houston an eerie silence surrounds all private space, the revenge of the holey plane. Here we are not talking about the voids left by leapfrogging or pockets of poverty, but the lack of a *public domain*. The silence is the sound of dross that in the final analysis must be compensated for by *something public*, space or otherwise. Even here in the hyperspace of the modern metropolis, an archipelago of isolated private spheres accessed solely by streets and highways seems untenable. It is clear that the same vigilance and optimism with which we embrace the global dimension must be applied to the local, but now exactly in the opposite direction.

The peculiar deadpan accessibility that exists in the gridded street pattern of the Museum District brings each museum a step closer to a public. The lack of zoning, the resulting absence of hierarchy, and the "accidental" juxtaposition of many uses add more openness, since you may stumble on a museum while on another errand. The nature of this *accidental field* has put museums next to hospitals, housing, restaurants, art galleries, houses, churches, and clinics, creating an alphabet soup of peculiar richness, variety, and openness. Yet museums remain "inaccessible." Lack of openness in Malraux's sense rather than accessibility may be the problem. The building block of the suburban metropolis is still *the pavilion in the park*, making the single-family house on its lot the basic model. Only lately have the museums begun to create on-site public space to promote openness to the street. This is an implicit acknowledgment that *public space* may still be needed to promote the open museum.

When Houston builds, it spends sixty percent of its $2 billion yearly budget on infrastructure, which means freeways, sewage, drainage, airports, a ball park (and a sprinkling of libraries, but not fiber optics or a public transportation system, for example). This confirms that getting in, around, and out is of primary concern in a world of radical mobility and efficient commerce. The commitment is to public networks but not to public space. Short of a major reorientation of the city's policies, public space will remain an abstraction, putting the issue back at the feet of the museums.

The aesthetic atmosphere of the museums operates along the metropolitan axis. Instant communication puts the museums closer to New York's MoMA than to the district itself. The depth of place has little relevance. The question of openness is therefore a complex cultural issue with some physical dimensions. Current museum policies, the endless rows of yellow school buses, blockbuster shows, and shopping-in-the-museum suggest that the directors are working on a "bridge to the public," compensating for the lack of automatic access inherent the traditional city's public realm.

It may seem ironic, in light of the optimism that pervades this book in relation to radical mobility, fluidity, change, even placelessness, and instant communication, that in the end the most direct solution to museum isolation is the call for a measure of pedestrian space best performed by traditional plazas and boulevards. But the terrain of the public realm in Houston and conurbations of a similar kind is no longer well symbolized by the colored squares of Mondrian's *Manhattan Boogie-Woogie*, but far more effectively by the colored drops in a Jackson Pollock drip painting. Public space happens wherever it can land. The underlying grammar of the suburban metropolis is atomization and fragmentation, and it is unproductive to resist this premise. The public realm must follow suit. But even this essentially physical reading is deceptive. "Public space" in the suburban metropolis is not the plaza of the city, but a peculiar blend of soft and hardware, more vapor than pavement, more dynamic than stable, because bound to events rather than manifested by places.

The key to the creation of a public dimension in the Museum District is to realize that the *local citizen*—the families of the working force of the global production apparatus—must be part of the museum world. The park associated with the Menil, or the sculpture garden at the Museum of Fine Arts, may have various publics (dog owners, wedding parties) that use them frequently but have yet to enter a museum. These kibbitzing publics may never be fully integrated, but, by existing side by side with museum-goers, they have the opportunity to be. Attempts to create assemblies of opportunity and simultaneity are central to openness. A basketball court next to the museum may help construct occasions in which the elegance of the game meets the beauty of paintings. This helps expand the notions of a "life in art." All these multiplicities are activity-driven. Time and occasion are more important than place.

The overall density of residential population, as distinct from event-provoked density, seems to be the destiny of each metropolitan region. Los Angeles is four times as dense as Houston, and it would take unimaginable political will to change this. However, in special districts, such as the Texas Medical Center and the Museum District, the Houston drift is toward increased residential density because of the externalities produced by the major activities. The current boom of multiple housing in Houston's inner loop is the market response to these "thickenings of the plot." Without public policy, the major actors must take the public domain into their own hands. In this light, the Museum District must think itself a *megashape* whose coherence and vibrancy are built from within *by fictionalizing its characteristics*. Intense cooperation between all involved is needed, but since the theme is already established, mobilizing the content of the fiction seems possible. An internal *spatial flow* must be constructed in which the blocks of the districts are brought together by software: blockbuster museum shows, metropolitan vapors: raves, stims, Foto Fests, fireworks, marathons, street fairs, sports events, music-in-the-streets, bike-ins, and political rallies, all cast in the vapor of museums.

The very genetics of the middle landscape, and the loose agglomerations of "similarities" (museums, hospitals, etc.) populating it, suggest strongly that the city government will be a minor player in any form of change. Instead the major institutions, in full view of the immediately affected community, must do the work. The aggressive museum building, and the proliferation of new "populist" museums, is promising, but the physical props building the "windows to the public" have yet to find engaging shapes and programs. Rather than relying on Menil's field theory of buildings and space as markers, the populist museums rely on stodgy familiarity and heavy marketing. The typical suburban one-liner rules the day: the flaccid canopy, the large banner, a clump of trees, and a bench to rest on, before and after. A new vocabulary of suburban communication devices needs to be developed relying less on permanence and more on the deliberate coincidence of the complex publics, the built, and the program. Rather than the old, the new Las Vegas may have to lead the way. A *transient permanence* may be the result, transient because as a stim it is turned on and off, permanent because it is repeated over and over again. Circus over city.

Frontier Ecology

The other side of the middle landscape, the wards of poverty, lies still as a downtown parking lot on Sunday. A century of programs designed to solve the endemic problem of poverty lies dormant. Today some seventy million people live in these pools of economic underdevelopment, in the nation's metropolises and beyond. Much like the voids in the holey plane, the wards, each with its own imbricated strata, do not participate in the prosperity of the Museum District. And judging by the wards' modern history, there is little hope for improvement. Like a public transportation system that skips a depressed area, the modern spatial flows are destined elsewhere. We can safely assume that some twenty percent of the population in the middle landscape is poor, under- or unemployed, poorly educated, and lives under precarious family conditions. The inner components of an ecology, if not its workings, may be best understood here.

The utter lack of political will and compassion are blatantly visible in some of the poorest wards. Massive public funds have been used repeatedly to destroy decent housing to disperse the population. Any attempts at cooperation between city and wards seem doomed to fail, although this is a crucial part of a functioning ecology. Self-improvement, another of the salient components, is almost impossible when there are no proximity groupings attracting resources and technology to start small enterprises. Data about social and economic conditions abound, but there are no devices to turn the data into useful information that may lead to enterprise and hope.

To build ecology is to build relationships: general ones such as with the city, schools, work, and leisure and specific and unique ones laden with emotion and character, as with family, relatives, community groups, and athletic teams. The city gives no assistance, no encouragement or incentives (free land, tax-free zones, interest-free loans, vouchers, etc.); only local churches, charities, and dedicated volunteers do. The schools are more than substandard, lacking any access to the outer world with all its wealth and technology. Like rusted, stalled engines, the wards of poverty are graphic expressions of dying ecology.

To approach this seemingly impossible task (outside the tax model) is to build what Manuel Castells calls *spatial flows*. The pockets of poverty are totally discon-nected from the spatial network in which information, knowledge, skill, and pro-duction flow. It is unlikely that such essential connections will be made unless the pockets have something to offer. Much like the frontier, these embryonic spatial flows are already on their own. To paraphrase Bacon, the light must be lit inside, fu-eled by science, a drive to discover affection and human emotion. The current state of the wards of poverty is living proof of the tragic consequence of underestimating the cultural dimension in the building of spatial flows and frontier ecologies. The looser, more ephemeral relationships in an assembly of men, women, and children building a production and community apparatus are as essential as the strong forces and frictions of the horse/men/bull/technology machine. Just as important as close relations among the working components of such an apparatus are the loose and ephemeral relationships with the global context of the ecology. The rea-sons are not just to build connections but to see these as crucial access points in making larger, more powerful external spatial flows. The principle is to break down barriers as well as building relations. Broken barriers widen the scope, without de-flecting the narrow purpose, and force various participants to work together. Never having become a deductive science, community-building remains a theoretical en-lightenment project, sadly stuck in the academy. The prospect of making the en-trepreneurial concept of spatial flows successful, socially and economically, seems equally dim.

Architecture and Biota

Nature, to be commanded, must be obeyed.
—Francis Bacon

We talk of deviations from natural life, as if artificial life were not also natural.
—Ralph Waldo Emerson

Renzo Piano, the architect of the Menil Collection, made a refracting and subtle move when he turned the Cy Twombly Gallery ninety degrees away from the street.

Against the common organization of the houses on the existing block, in which all entrances face the street, the gallery opens onto a lawn in which a grand oak tree presides.

Just as he rearranged the Jeffersonian university grammar in the placement of the large museum on its lawn, Piano manipulated, in the placement of the Twombly, the demanding and rigid logic of the regular city block, leaving an inner sanctum relegated to nature. The decision to turn away from the street, the traffic, and direct vehicular access may have been made to establish the difference between house and museum, to put distance between contemplation and action, and to turn visitors, ever so briefly, into pedestrians. However rational and coolly elegant the ninety-degree move, it was also a radical move from a metropolitan perspective, a *turning* of the quintessential urban museum toward the inside of the block to consolidate with nature. With this rotation away from the mercantile toward the agrarian, the new museum joins forces with the zoohemic canopy.

As difficult as the construction of spatial flows may seem, the reinvention of architecture for the suburban metropolis is even more difficult. Clearly, as the double expression of the architect's and the client's private proclivity, architecture is doing well. And it has a well-established market. But I am referring to architecture of consequence, the kind that used to build the cities of the past: architecture as a public good. The museum colluding with the canopy of trees is the embryo of such a good.

This thought, this ambition, might never have occurred had I not kept returning to the zoohemic canopy, to the trees, to the biota, the animal and plant life of the middle landscape. Between winter and spring, the canopy ranges in color from a pale purple to intense green, from dormant to fully alive. This process of sleep and awakening brings to the middle landscape its natural splendor, but more pragmatically it reflects the flow of energy, the power of climate, and marks the passages in the yearly cycle. The biota sets the manners of the seasons and defines the horizon of the complex middle ecology.

Obliquely there is a deep commitment to the zoohemic canopy in the middle landscape. The leapfrogged holes in the urban fabric contribute significantly and as accidentally to the sporadic maintenance of the canopy. As with so many complexes in the suburban metropolis, the canopy is on its own assignment. Its support of and integration with these other systems (streets, housing, public space) often seem accidental and haphazard. When it does support these systems, it does so as a matter of fact, as something metropolitans take for granted, out of focus in the corner of their daily perceptions. Yet the biota counteracts, balances, and often hides the rampant artifice. (Landscape architects as camouflage artists, called in when architect and developer have finished, know this all too well.) In our everyday lives we see the gardens, the trees, the birds, and the bayou snakes as pleasant surplus to the real estate. Yet without them we would realize that they establish and embody the radical difference between the metropolis and the city. Consequently, if we looked at the *bios* as the *ethos* of suburban culture and artifice as its poor relation (not yet) working hard to become as intelligent and alive, *architecture might again find its purpose*. Even when winter or bulldozers suppress it, the biota would again come into focus, no longer as an adverse and threatening wilderness but as the conceptual locus of the suburban metropolis.

The great oak tree facing the Twombly Gallery gains presence and specificity by its privileged placement. When visitors exit the museum they see a great oak rather than a motor vehicle. But its nature is of greater potential and consequence. If we fail to see the individual tree for the canopy, we may also miss the immense bayou system that delineates the plane and miss its role in the service of the tree. The tree working as a huge pump gets its water molecules from the ground and releases them via its leafed crown into the atmosphere at the time of photosynthesis. All is driven by solar power. This cycle is a form of *stimdross*, in which the visible and apparently significant reveals its dependence on the less apparent. And there are millions of these trees, pumping away; and unlike their artificial others pumping oil, the trees' output is clean. The conceptual and technical distance between these two pumps is unlikely to be bridged any time soon. But since architects are more susceptible to change, what can we learn from trees?[11]

The turning of a museum toward a tree is without any consequence on the metropolitan scale, while here on a microscopic scale the wild has won over the west, an implosion has taken place. The frontier is now within the metropolis.

■

The double movement—the turn toward the canopy and the simultaneous mimesis[12] between canopy and roof—is an exquisite demonstration of the biota as the conceptual center of a new metropolis. The *turning* of the suburban metropolis toward nature neither implies a turning *away* from what de Certeau called "the universal writing of technology" nor a return to some new version of the picturesque, but a *dragging* (as with assistance of a computer mouse) in which culture and nature become coexistent multiplicities. One is seen through the other. The turning toward nature does not suggest that culture should be an extension or prolongation of nature, but that coexistence would provoke a mimesis and a shoal of interactivity. Innovation and market forces cannot be replaced by some newfangled rootedness. Rather all three must find their way and expression through various processes of reconciliation. The new nature is no longer the dauntingly opaque wilderness that the Puritans encountered, but an emerging evolutionary complex in which we as *creatures of matter*[13]—and our technological extensions—are implicated.

The *hint* of nature that Piano constructed in the glass canopy in the Twombly Gallery is a trace that traveled a long way. Gilles Deleuze writes in reference to Bergson's philosophy of matter, memory, and duration:

> Thus, when life is divided into plant and animal, when the animal is divided into instinct and intelligence, each side of the division, each ramification, carries the whole with it. From a certain perspective it is like an accompanying nebulosity, testifying to its undivided origin. And there is a halo of instinct in intelligence, a nebula of intelligence in instinct, a hint of the animate in plants, and of the vegetable in animals.[14]

By extension and implication—scaling high conceptual walls, traveling across vast homogeneous and normally closed territories—the *vegetable*, via man's *animality*, has infiltrated his technology. No longer a mere thought or ambition, the glass canopy in the museum embodies the surrounding canopy of trees. The age of integration has begun.

■

The bull machine in the Feria of Nîmes, deep in the Camargue of southern France, relied on *proximity* for its success, indeed for its *beauty*. Seen from within the bull run, with my young son on my shoulders, just at the outset (presumably a safe distance from the bull's potential outbreak), the faces, the clothing, and the posture of the riders are etched in my memory—a strangely beautiful tableau—a Velásquez on the run. Heads raised, proudly, knowingly, bodies erect but leaning in on the bull; pride, strength, the bullfighters' *machismo*; yet when these are combined with everyday clothes—an Adidas shirt, worn boots, the typical Camargue moleskin riding pants with colored piping—the here and now slips in to bring the real down to us, the bull's potential prey. Over by the bull like the albumen of an egg, the riders protect and harbor their power as joined and displaced in the bull. This decenteredness shifts the attention from the egos of men and from the powers and fury of bulls to some separate and, in terms of consequence, larger in-between. This is an action in which men are *becoming* animals, and vice versa. "A nebulosity of instinct and intelligence" hovers here. This halo, this in-between, is the locus of architecture, away from egos and power, in place and time, during an event, in a "form-preserving instability," in the very "fever of matter," to borrow from Frederick Turner and to paraphrase Thomas Mann.[15]

The key to the fever is proximity, particularly when seen against the panorama of U.S. distance. From the tense proximity between Puritans and the wilderness to the hesitant proximity between technology and nature, *distance* remains at the center. The future of architecture lies at the heart of the struggle for distance. Proximity, or more precisely contiguity, made the fabric of the city, and again proximity and contiguity reappear but now in a very different mien: architecture, like all artifice, must through "hints and halos" embody nature. Both have to get closer, and both would in this becoming be reinvented.

A proposition for a new metropolis may seem audacious, particularly when the central pivot is the merging of nature and artifice, a subject hardly at the center of everyday life. Yet such attention to the most lofty may not be entirely foolhardy. Claude Lévi-Strauss wrote in his *Tristes Tropiques* of 1974:

> The major manifestations of social life have something in common with works of art, namely that they come into being on the level of the unconscious, because they are collective, although works of art are individual. However, this is a minor difference, and really only an apparent one, since social phenomena are produced by the public and works of

art for the public; it is the public which endows them with a common de-
nominator and determines the conditions of their creation.

So it is not in any metaphorical sense that we are justified in comparing—as has often been done—a town with a symphony or a poem;
they are objects of a similar nature. The town is perhaps even more pre-
cious than a work of art in that it stands at the meeting point of nature
and artifice. Consisting, as it does, of a community of animals who enclose their biological history within the boundaries and at the same time
mould it according to their every intention as thinking beings, the town,
in both its development and its form, belongs simultaneously to biological procreation, organic evolution and aesthetic creation. It is at one
and the same time an object of nature and a subject of nature; an individual and a group; reality and dream; the supremely human achievement.[16]

At the verge of the twenty-first century, the supremely human achievement has
a dark side: culture's slow but steady destruction of the environment, as reflected
in global warming and persistent pollution of air, land, and stream. The turning toward nature in the metropolis may be the first step toward this immense project and
the beginning of the century of the environment.

■

Opaque, the dense spring foliage of a million trees hides the floor of the metropolis. Only the downtown towers thumb through. When at the outset of this book I
looked out over this scene, it appeared excited and in constant flux, although at
that time there was very little building. Now the scene appears transfixed, immobile, yet it is bustling with activity, as hundreds of new housing units are being built
in the green voids below. This contradiction between apparent stillness and actual
construction is a reflection of a perplexing stalemate, of a crisis of will in the face of
apparent ability.

Seemingly frozen in their bottom-line conception, the new housing estates may
be the result of ultimate efficiency, "appropriate" technology, economy, speed, and
construction ability. Yet they are petrified in their banality. Blind to their surround-

ings, insensible to the climate, ignorant of anything but the most stereotypical habitation, forming automatic enclaves because of their rigid uniformity, these buildings betray the intelligence of a metropolis world-renowned for its advanced medicine, forward-looking science, creative oil exploration, and enormous economic vigor. The rigor mortis is completed by the employment of out-of-date building styles (Georgian and Mediterranean)—the lethal combination of stereotypical architectural representations and a highly proficient building and sales machinery. The roots of this collusion are complex. It is hardly the result of a sinister conspiracy, rather the coincidence of a deep-seated conservatism on the part of dwellers and makers and the drift of the market system, most notably the mortgage industry. It is deeply ironic that Adolf Loos's comment on the Austrian bourgeoisie of the 1930s—"The work of art is radical and the house is conservative"—is reborn here in one of the most modern and demographically diverse manifestations of very late twentieth-century urban culture. History will determine whether it is a tragedy or a farce, particularly since the mortgage bankers' conservatism is often conveniently blamed. Bankers follow the market, and markets are not entirely constructed, which in turn leads back to the dweller. A dweller whose specific professional sophistication is exceptional but whose cultural commitment seems murky, if not repressed; a distant misty England comes to mind, replete with Georgians and Land Rovers.

The spectacular growth of the suburban metropolis, of which Houston is a typical example, has resulted in a giant board game—the *cordon urbain*—in which nature and culture are running side by side, one oblivious of the other. Conservative values and smoothly operating machineries from real estate to transportation form alliances of enormous efficiency and strength. Architects have excluded themselves from the game. Yet all is not well. The deep-seated denial of the larger consequences of all accumulated actions has produced a holey plane with too many voids of social and economic depression, serious environmental problems, and often banal and overly striated spatial stereotypes. This refusal misses countless opportunities to pool resources, to build new and more diverse coalitions, and to construct richer and more complex environmental conditions. Such radical rearrangements—a new alliance—will be essential to our prosperity. Suburban culture will no longer be rescued by the city's.

Proliferating in the voids of the middle landscape, the housing estates close down the new urban frontier. In theory there is only one part to replace in an im-

mensely delicate machinery, and the direction of this seemingly inevitable development could be reversed. The missing part is the salient part, the key to the design
machine, the part that bridges the heterogeneous—the *vegetable* in the inanimate,
the *hint* that makes a building cognizant of a larger plane: climate, biota, complex
dweller needs, various economies, alternative styles and predilections. Yet the
hope of inserting the missing link in the design machine is slim.

However, since *time* is on the side of the zoohemic ecology, the next generation—my students—may defy the various suburban machineries and insert the
missing link because they already know that the abyss between technology and
nature must be bridged. As the psychologist Richard Korn said: "There will be a
time when our children will teach us."[17] May that time be very soon. And time is of
the essence, because when we leave the city behind, we have left space behind. If
the second law of thermodynamics applies, the city's architectonic order has been
replaced by entropy.

In the metropolis there is only time.

■

Driving aimlessly along the byways under the zoohemic canopy, avoiding the des-
tination-prone freeway, the drifter can only wonder about place. In the suburban
metropolis space is unbound and places are evenly spaced. Place, tightly defined,
is paradoxically everywhere. Yet place, as in a sense of place, is bound to the
stim—place *takes place* only.

Almost smooth, almost nomadic, suburban space appears endless (Houston is
everywhere!). Yet events take place, even when unseen by the drifter, and simultaneously, thus saturating the holey plane with place. For extended moments the performance of place stops the endless. In the 1960s, Melvin Webber, the University
of California planning professor, wrote of "community without propinquity," where
performed networks bind together a myriad of dispersed places, defying the assumed loss of community (the city). But what will the further *smoothing* of space
mean? When we *fuse* nature, in its old position as space, and culture, as in place
(in its old position as nature's binary opposite), will the result be fewer places and
more space? Or will we have more time in a very large and endless place? Will we
then be immersed in an endless stim?

We used not to see the forest for the trees. What happens when we cannot see the houses for the forest? And the body. Will it too disappear in the forest? And as Foucault suggested, will humans be erased "like a face drawn on the beach"—but now in favor of the humanized energies of the electronic forest?

■

On the freeway, the mood is different. Standing above it, the flow of the morning commuter traffic is steady. Looking closer, there are oscillations. Around me, Pascal Rogé plays Erik Satie's *Gymnopédie N.2*, Sparta's dance to Apollo, but instead of agile boys, the sleek metallic bodies of cars perform. Rarely cars align across the four lanes, and when three cars do, they stay together for a second only: a certain distance at work, independence and cooperation.[18] Six to seven cars slide back and forth inside my focus, held apart by mutual and mild aversion, while being held together by proxemics: the product of car size, lane width, freeway geometry, speed, habit, rules, and surveillance. A dance, a swarming, motorized prowess celebrating a new Apollo. Sparta may have had its revenge on the city right here on the superhighway, but the drifters' apparent directional resolve leading to a common destiny beyond my vision is deceiving. They will all disperse. Purportedly Satie told Debussy to get rid of his Wagnerisms by taking the sauerkraut out of his music. Beyond the revenge, and in defiance of their dispersed destinations, the metropolitans must similarly erase the city and (loosely) unite to seek a new destiny.

Notes

I Introduction

1.   Manfredo Tafuri, *Architecture and Utopia: Design and Capitalist Development,* trans. Barbara Luigia La Penta (Cambridge: MIT Press, 1976), p. 43.

2.   Ibid., p. 42.

3.   Gianni Vattimo, *The End of Modernity: Nihilism and Hermeneutics in Postmodern Culture,* trans. Jon R. Snyder (Baltimore: Johns Hopkins University Press, 1991), p. 1. Particularly the concept of *Verwindung*.

4.   The idea of *growing our house* stems from a disparate range of sources, from Marvin Minsky's *Society of Mind*, to Luc Ferry's critique of deep ecology, to Frederick Turner's "Biology and Beauty," to the environmental crisis and its management.

5.   Tafuri, *Architecture and Utopia*, pp. 16, 19.

6.   Ibid., p. 18.

7.   Ibid., p. 24.

8.   Ibid.

9.   Ibid., p. 26.

10.   Ibid.

11.   Walter Benjamin, *Reflections: Essays, Aphorisms, Autobiographical Writings,* ed. Peter Demetz, trans. Edmund Jephcott (New York: Harcourt Brace Jovanovich, 1978), p. 43.

12.   It should be noted that Lenin had but "scorn for the life of the masses"; in Michel Maffesoli's *The Time of the Tribes: The Decline of Individualism in Mass Society,* trans. Don Smith (London: Sage Publications, 1996), p. 154.

13.   William L. MacDonald, *The Pantheon: Design, Meaning, and Progeny* (Cambridge: Harvard University Press, 1976).

14.   Michel Serres, *Rome: The Book of Foundations,* trans. Felicia McCarren (Stanford: Stanford University Press, 1991), p. 62.

15.   Ibid., p. 64.

16.   Ibid.

17.   Michel Foucault, *The Order of Things: An Archaeology of the Human Sciences* (New York: Random House, 1970), pp. 9–10.

18. Michel Foucault, *Discipline and Punish: The Birth of the Prison*, trans. Alan Sheridan (New York: Random House, 1979), p. 216.

19. Ibid.

20. Ibid., p. 217.

21. Ibid., p. 201.

22. Ibid., p. 208.

23. Georges Bataille, quoted in Denis Hollier, *Against Architecture: The Writings of Georges Bataille,* trans. Betsy Wing (Cambridge: MIT Press, 1989), p. 47.

24. Ibid.

25. Aldo Rossi, *The Architecture of the City* (Cambridge: MIT Press, 1982), p. 60.

26. Hollier, *Against Architecture*, p. 55.

27. Bataille, quoted in Hollier, *Against Architecture*, p. 53.

28. Hollier, *Against Architecture*, p. 47.

29. Ibid., p. xii.

30. The Latin inscription aside, historians seem to agree that the most likely architect is Hadrian.

31. Walter Benjamin, *Illuminations: Essays and Reflections,* ed. Hannah Arendt, trans. Harry Zohn (New York: Schocken Books, 1969), pp. 239–241.

32. Hollier, *Against Architecture*, p. xiii.

33. Ibid.

34. Rossi, *The Architecture of the City,* p. 18. Rossi defines *fabbrica* as "building" in the old Latin and Renaissance sense of man's construction as it continues over time. The Milanese still call their cathedral "la fabbrica del dom," and understand by this expression both the difficulty of the church's construction and the idea of a building whose process goes on over time.

35. Norman Bryson, "The Gaze in the Expanded Field," in Hal Foster, ed., *Vision and Visuality* (Seattle: Bay Press, 1988), p. 87.

36. Ibid.

37. The point about imagination should be stressed here, since I have yet to visit the gap. This is not entirely due to lack of opportunity, but rather in order to keep the gap imaginary for as long as possible. A visit will eventually be necessary because, I have been told, gazing

down through the oculus is one of the great architectural experiences.

38. Bryson, "The Gaze in the Expanded Field," p. 110.

39. Henri Focillon, *The Life of Forms in Art,* trans. Charles Beecher Hogan and George Kubler (New York: Zone Books, 1989), p. 61.

40. Ibid., p. 35.

41. Ibid., p. 36.

42. Bryson, "The Gaze in the Expanded Field," p. 103.

43. Hollier, *Against Architecture*, p. xi.

44. Ibid., pp. 32–33.

45. Jacques Derrida, *Of Grammatology,* trans. Gayatri Chakravorty Spivak (Baltimore: Johns Hopkins University Press, 1976).

46. Roland Barthes, *The Pleasure of the Text*, trans. Richard Miller (New York: Hill & Wang, 1975), p. 9.

II The Suburban Metropolis

An earlier version of "Stim and Dross: Rethinking the Metropolis" was published in *Assemblage* (Cambridge: MIT Press, 1994), pp. 82–100.

1. The city we face at the dusk of the century is infinitely more complex than the night suggests. We must close the book on the City and open the manifold of the Metropolis. Behind this melodramatic pronouncement lies the hypothesis that our customary ways of describing, managing, and designing the city are now outmoded. Though the world is mutating at a dizzying speed, we remain mesmerized by the *passéiste* dream of the City. Contemporary metropolitans must confront a series of givens that radically change the equation of the old city. Perhaps nowhere with more intensity than in Houston is the full set of these revolutions being cinematically played out: *Demographic*: in the emerging metropolis, the old patterns are giving way to a truly multiethnic continuum. *Economic*: global integration threatens not only to extend but to continuously redraw the boundaries of the city's hinterland. *Domestic*: both parents have absented themselves from the household semipermanently to enter the marketplace, despite and because of chronic and massive unemployment, while in the shadows hover AIDS, homelessness, substance abuse, and epidemic violence. *Resources:* emphasis has shifted from raw and manufactured materials to "immaterials" such as knowledge, services, management. *Ecology:* a science, a politics, and an ethics that is no longer a fad. (Drawn from a lecture by Stephen L. Klineberg, "Making Sense of Our Times: Five Revolutionary Trends.")

2.   The entire section on the relationship between physics and the metropolis is drawn from Martin Krieger's *Doing Physics: How Physicists Take Hold of the World* (Bloomington: Indiana University Press, 1992), p. 25.

3.   Walter Benjamin, "Theses on the Philosophy of History," in *Illuminations: Essays and Reflections,* ed. Hannah Arendt, trans. Harry Zohn (New York: Schocken Books, 1969), pp. 257–258.

4.   Paul Cummings, "Interview with Robert Smithson for the Archives of American Art/Smithsonian Institution," in *The Writings of Robert Smithson* (New York: New York University Press, 1979), p. 154.

5.   Kevin Lynch's work in *The Image of the City* (Cambridge, Mass.: Technology Press, 1960) on cognitive mapping, in which he distinguishes "districts, nodes, landmarks, edges and paths," prefigures notions such as the megashape. The radical difference is that he concentrated on mapping techniques, while the megashape probably found its inspiration in cinematography. Someone may find it fruitful to marry the two.

6.   At night the disembodied city reveals itself. Especially during the holidays when the wattage is radically increased as each building is lit like a Christmas tree. This custom may have been learned from Las Vegas, whose casino operators are known to create highs with a mixture of light and oxygen. Presumably the Houston version is meant to induce shopping euphoria. From the 28th floor, the towers of downtown glow in their priapic elegance, while 120 degrees due west the spread-out buildings of the Galleria, accented with horizontal bars of light running along the eaves, highlight their low-slung horizontality. As two ends of a spectrum displaced by a *certain distance*, the separation (at birth) between the vertical and the horizontal is eerily graphic. The decision to remove the commercial ground-floor business from downtown and to relocate it on the grounds of the Galleria is the most dramatic display of the demise of the city and the rise of the metropolis. The instigators, Gerald Hines and his real estate movers, did in one single Monopoly move what Alexander may have achieved by chopping off the Gordian knot. Those nostalgic for the city that could have been are still smarting. For the suburbanite the logic was clear: with the separation of the oil business from shopping, the male would get his world and the female hers. In the process we would avoid congestion, traffic snarls, parking problems, street life, all the components that make up the inefficient and wicked twentieth-century downtown. Nostalgic attempts to return downtown to Downtown are not only futile but ill advised, since they obscure the fact that Houston is not a city but a multicentered metropolitan domain in which each center has to fend for itself. In other words, when Houston Industries lights up downtown in a huge multimillion-dollar firework, they are much closer to a more productive strategy: as a potential contender as energy capital of the world, Houston's downtown needs to be in a perpetual light high; only then will it be able to fictionalize its true characteristics. In the meantime the third-world surface of downtown, occupied by service workers, derelicts, and other marginals, is carefully avoided by the vertical axis of the members of the first world, who slip into their elevators, out through their underground tunnels to the parking lot, via the freeway to their home-sweet-home only

a gallon of gas away. This part of downtown's horizontality was left behind to linger in the shadows of the remaining towers.

7.   It is ironic, at the end of a century characterized by the most dizzying urban transformations in human history, that academic readings (apart from writers like Banham and Koolhaas) and projects of the city (particularly in postwar cities like Houston) remain haunted by the irrelevant ghost of the historically outdated European city center. A distinctly European view of our cities makes them embattled, ridiculed, and flat—too often conceived as mere Monopoly games. The hegemony of the pedestrian, the plaza, the street, and the perimeter block must be challenged not because the values they embody are no longer valid, but because they are suffused with a set of fundamental misconceptions about the nature of contemporary civilization and its *outside*, leading to a false understanding of the whole. More pointedly, even the most sophisticated readings (and the occasional building) of the American city and its postwar expansions, whether haunted and paranoid (as in Baudrillard's *America*) or openly nostalgic for the eternal return of the bourgeois pedestrian (Krier, Duany and Plater-Zyberk, Calthorpe, Solomon), are predicated upon a more or less hidden positivity that, if fulfilled, would bring us community—or better, bring us back to the American version of the European city. Yet the city is forever surpassed by the metropolis and all its givens (a steadily globalizing economy, demographic changes, AIDS, unemployment, and violence), all of which will make any return to the past impossible and undesirable. The obsession with valorizing the pedestrian over the car hides the fact that there is a driver (and passengers) in the car—a roving subjectivity whose body phantom apprehends the world in a vastly different manner, a manner that in turn will and must have consequences for the way the metropolis is designed. More important, however, to hinge all judgments about the city on the forlorn pedestrian and all his requirements avoids tackling the fact that the metropolis is driven in and driven not only by the pedestrian and the driver but by a myriad of subjectivities ranging from the old (and possibly infirm) to the young (and equally vulnerable), men and women, African-American and white, as well as less human objectivities such as the economy, public opinion, and the marketplace.

8.   The stabilities of the old city, its buildings, monuments, and city fabric, are rapidly losing their firmness (if not their delight). Buildings in cities like Tokyo and Houston are likely to disappear before their mortgages run out and long before the companies that occupy them. New street systems are broken, cul-de-sac-ed, and largely incoherent, leading somewhere but never everywhere. Monuments, often built for enormous sums of money, are completely idiosyncratic and out of date. Because they serve so few, their publication in various media is more consequential than the monuments themselves. In the metropolis, absurdly, shockingly, a series of radical reversals of stability have taken place. Aspects and characteristics that in the city were the mere backdrop of everyday life have been rudely foregrounded as new stabilities: stabilities that are not characterized by their firmness but rather by their dynamic, unpredictable instability. I am thinking about pollution, weather, vegetation, and water. None of these is, under the demanding auspices of the metropolis, truly natural, but a complex compound or admixture of nature and artifice. Yet in their persistent return or foregrounding, we know that they all will be here when we leave. Despite often valiant attempts to reverse its presence, pollution is here to stay. It will come and go; if one type is held back, pollution as a

fixture of metropolitan life will return, be it in the air, water, food, or our bodies. Pollution slows imperceptibly between nature and artifice. And on the side of artifice flow other stable instabilities, such as electricity and gas and their transformation into lights and vehicles. The "astral specs" of the artificially lit metropolis bring the entire conurbation under the same spell at night. It is as if nocturnally the metropolis counts itself, one light for every event. Traffic flows, peaking twice a day, are as predictable as the profile of downtown. Yet this flow is also highly unstable. This goes for weather, vegetation, and water—particularly true in Houston, where the water table often shows its sudden destructive power on the ground floor of the city—the sudden liberation of all bathtub rubber ducks. Sooner or later these instabilities will bring all of us into their momentary orbits. The nature of all these new stabilities is their catastrophic instability, their dynamic flux, which like the metropolis itself immerse everyday life in their only semi-predictable power games—semi-natural or semi-artificial. When the rainstorm, the morning commute, the steady TV signal, and the open telephone line—and lately, bandwidth—have become our only stability, the city as we have known it has truly disappeared. *Firmitas* has become stochastic and conjectural.

9.   Smithson, *Writings of Robert Smithson*, p. 55.

10.   The city must be seen as an organism, but as such a deeply perplexing one because it is simultaneously a machine, or rather a series of disconnected (nano-)machines running their own determined and reckless courses—the combined results of which we will never fully fathom. Drifting, the procedure of preference for this reading, is umbilically connected to the metropolis, via Baudelaire and the ultimate *flâneur* Walter Benjamin (although he would agree that in Houston the car rather than pedestrian locomotion is the drifter's vehicle par excellence). Benjamin began his drifting across the metropolis on the back porch overlooking the inner court of his parents' apartment in Berlin. Here he had his first encounters with the Other and learned that the bright lights of the city are not only lights but tokens of the many pistons that drive its motors—the multitude of languages at work—whether under his bedroom door (when his emancipated Jewish parents entertained friends on Saturday night) or the mesmerizing red light signaling the prostitution district. Despite the semantic luminosity of the many city lights, there is no sense that Benjamin finds anything but tensions, ruptures, and catastrophic leaps. The more he seems to grasp the metropolis, the faster he sees it slip away, until he finally escapes, by his own hand, in distant Port-Bou.

This text is ostensibly a drift along Houston's many physical trajectories. Like gossip or commentary, the many oddities and kinks on the hide of this otherwise·"lite city" (Koolhaas) lead to descriptions that warp and bend, while making the physical reverberate with all the other not-so-physical frameworks and constructions that shape the metropolis, ranging from the House to the Office to the circulation of Money. Drifting-as-text is more about departures than arrivals, more about movement and change than fixedness, but also about a desire to cover more with less, a leaving of lacunas to be filled later with the help of others.

11.   The term *subecology* applies to large domains in Houston, but a narrower band can be defined that roughly surrounds downtown and reaches out to the first beltway—an example of the middle landscape.

12.   The holes, "the empty lots," writes Michael Benedikt, "dotted about the landscape [have] to do with the use of land as speculative investment vehicle[s] by banks, real estate investment trusts [REITS], and even individuals, with deep enough pockets to wait for more favorable . . . market conditions." Quoted in Michael Storper, "Beautiful Cities, Ugly Cities: Urban Form as Convention," in *Center* 10, ed. Michael Benedikt (Austin: Center for the Study of American Architecture, University of Texas at Austin, 1997), p. 122.

13.   Jean Baudrillard, *America,* trans. Chris Turner (New York: Verso, 1988), p. 27.

14.   Ibid., p. 105.

15.   Ibid., p. 7.

16.   The two dominating ecologies harbor a multitude of subecologies or biotopes (limited ecological regions or niches in which the environment promotes and supports certain forms of life). These *topoi* are often the growing grounds for the stim, whose *biotic potential* (the likelihood of survival of a specific organism in a specific environment, especially in an unfavorable one) is, as I hope to show, highly dependent on both stim and surrounding dross.

17.   J. B. Jackson, "The Westward-Moving House," in *Landscapes: Selected Writing of J. B. Jackson,* ed. Erwin H. Zube (Amherst: University of Massachusetts Press, 1970), p. 10.

18.   "In the Entortung it is the destiny of the West itself that runs from the rooting of the *Nomos* in the *justissima tellus,* through the discovery and occupation of the new spaces of the Americas ('free' spaces, that is, considered totally available for conquest, totally profanable: devoid of places), up to the universalism of the world market . . . (a total mobilization of an intensive kind, a universal displacement)." Massimo Cacciari, *Architecture and Nihilism: On the Philosophy of Modern Architecture,* trans. Stephen Sartarelli (New Haven: Yale University Press, 1993), p. 169.

19.   The issue of appropriateness is evident here. However, the complexity and multitude of cultures and concerns in the manifold of the metropolis force us to seriously question contextualism, or to elevate this issue to *environmental contextuality,* leaving the issue of style to the beholder.

20.   The stim's apparent mixture of program and building on the one hand and all the support structures (people and machines) on the other makes evident that the designer can but maybe should not exclude the latter from the design equation. Interior designers frequently cross the line between hardware and software. This attitude becomes even more relevant when environmental issues are brought up, since they have direct bearing on the life cycle and life span of the building (and all its elements and systems) and thus directly with its life (use).

21.   In attempting to find a narrow definition of the stim, I have at this point excluded the workplace, although, clearly stimming takes place here too. The subject of the *suburbanization of work* and the increased need for stims to compensate for the *loss of the office* is a chapter in itself, in need of extensive exploration.

22. Hannah Arendt, *The Human Condition* (Chicago: University of Chicago Press, 1958), pp. 22–35.

23. Most notably, Duany and Plater-Zyberk, and just recently the Disney Company.

24. The Open City is a code for the democratic city, accessible by a complete grid—the good city in my book.

25. David Bell, "Knowledge and the Middle Landscape: Jefferson's University of Virginia," *Journal of Architectural Education,* 37, no. 2 (Winter 1983), pp. 18–26.

26. Ibid., p. 18.

27. Thomas Jefferson as quoted in Bell, "Knowledge and the Middle Landscape," p. 22.

28. Alexander Tzonis and Liane Lefaivre, *Classical Architecture: The Poetics of Order* (Cambridge: MIT Press, 1986), p. 9.

29. Thomas Jefferson quoted in Bell, "Knowledge and the Middle Landscape," p. 25.

30. Bell, "Knowledge and the Middle Landscape," p. 21.

31. Lecture at University of California, Department of Geography, Fall 1967.

32. Grady Clay, *Real Places: An Unconventional Guide to America's Generic Landscape* (Chicago: University of Chicago Press, 1994), p. xx.

33. E. T. Hall, *The Hidden Dimension* (New York: Anchor Books, 1990).

34. Perry Miller, *Errand into the Wilderness* (Cambridge: Harvard University Press, 1956), p. 3.

35. Ibid.

36. Ibid., p. 216.

37. Manfredo Tafuri, *Architecture and Utopia: Design and Capitalist Development*, trans. Barbara Luigia La Penta (Cambridge: MIT Press, 1976), p. 125.

38. Félix Guattari, *Chaosophy* (New York: Semiotext(e), 1995), p. 41.

39. Philip Guedalla, *The Hundred Years* (New York: Torch Books, 1936), p. 38.

40. Luc Ferry, *The New Ecological Order,* trans. Carol Volk (Chicago: University of Chicago Press, 1995), p. 64.

41. Donald Judd, *Architektur* (Münster: Westf'lisher Kunstverein, 1989).

42. Ibid., p. 26.

43. Ibid., pp. 65–66.

44.   Ibid., p. 66 (quoting Ortega y Gasset).

45.   Ibid., p. 79.

III Architecture Reconsidered

Some parts of "The End of the Architectural Promenade" were published in an earlier version in Scott Marble et al., eds., *Architecture and Body* (New York: Rizzoli, 1988), no pagination.

Scattered fragments of "The Metropolitan Architect" were published as "Hands Up," in *Louis I. Kahn: Conversations with Students*, ed. Dung Ngo, Architecture @ Rice 26 (Houston: Rice School of Architecture, 1988), pp. 69–77.

1.   Walter Benjamin, *Illuminations: Essays and Reflections,* ed. Hannah Arendt, trans. Harry Zohn (New York: Schocken Books, 1969), pp. 239–241.

2.   The intimate connection between the Beaux-Arts dual concept of *enfilade/marche* and architectural promenade is most interesting. Based on David Van Zanten's comments in "Architectural Composition at the Ecole des Beaux-Arts: From Charles Percier to Charles Garnier," in Arthur Drexler, ed., *The Architecture of the Ecole des Beaux-Arts* (New York: Museum of Modern Art, 1977), there seems to be a direct link between *enfilade* and architecture and between *marche* and promenade—further investigation is called for.

3.   "Man of the Month: Le Corbusier," *Scope Magazine* (London), August 1951, pp. 67–68.

4.   Le Corbusier and Pierre Jeanneret, *Oeuvre complète de 1910–1929* (Zurich: Girsberger, 1937), p. 24. The French text reads: "L'auto s'engage sous les pilotis, tourne autour des services communs, arrive au milieu, à la porte du vestibule, entre dans le garage ou poursuit sa route pour le retour: telle est la donnée fondamentale."

5.   Ibid. The French text reads: "La maison se posera au milieu de l'herbe comme un objet, sans rien déranger."

6.   Ibid. The French text reads: "Mais on continue la promenade. Depuis le jardin à l'étage, on monte par la rampe sur le toit de la maison où est le solarium."

7.   Ibid. The French text reads: "L'architecture arabe nous donne un enseignement précieux. Elle s'apprécie à la marche, avec le pied; c'est en marchant, en se déplaçant que l'on voit se développer les ordonnances de l'architecture. C'est un principe contraire à l'architecture baroque qui est conçue sur le papier, autour d'un point fixe théorique. Je préfère l'enseignement de l'architecture arabe.

"Dans cette maison-ci, il s'agit d'une véritable promenade architecturale, offrant des aspects constamment variés, inattendus, parfois étonnants."

8.   Of the Villa Savoye Le Corbusier writes: "By the pilotis one ascends surreptitiously via a ramp, a sensation totally different from one of a stair formed by steps. A stair separates one story from another: a ramp connects." Le Corbusier and Pierre Jeanneret, *Oeuvre complète de 1929–1934* (Zurich: Girsberger, 1941), p. 25.

9.   Since the Plan Obus is utopia manifested, we no longer need the promise (as in the hope implied by the suspended garden), since, as Tafuri writes, "the technological universe is impervious to the here and there." Manfredo Tafuri, *Architecture and Utopia: Design and Capitalist Development,* trans. Barbara Luigia La Penta (Cambridge: MIT Press, 1976), p. 125.

10.   Lars Lerup, *Planned Assaults: The Nofamily House, Love/House, Texas Zero* (Montreal: Centre Canadien d'Architecture/Canadian Centre for Architecture, 1987), p. 16.

11.   Lars Lerup, *Building the Unfinished: Architecture and Human Action* (Beverly Hills: Sage Publications, 1977; out of print). This work covers in considerable detail my abandoning of behaviorism in favor of an activist perspective on the relation between dwellers and their physical world.

12.   Benjamin, *Illuminations,* p. 197.

13.   Jorge Luis Borges, *Labyrinths: Selected Stories and Other Writings,* ed. Donald A. Yates and James E. Irby (New York: New Directions, 1964), pp. 110–111.

14.   Umberto Eco, *A Theory of Semiotics* (Bloomington: Indiana University Press, 1979), p. 264.

15.   Arthur Quinn, *Figures of Speech: Sixty Ways to Turn a Phrase* (Berkeley: Hermagoras Press, 1993), pp. 42–44.

16.   Borges, *Labyrinths,* p. 26.

17.   Henri Lefebvre, *The Production of Space,* trans. Donald Nicholson-Smith (Oxford: Blackwell, 1991), p. 137.

18.   Maurice Merleau-Ponty, *Phenomenology of Perception,* trans. Colin Smith (London: Routledge & Kegan Paul, 1962), pp. 68–69.

19.   Michel de Certeau, *The Practice of Everyday Life,* trans. Steven F. Rendall (Berkeley: University of California Press, 1984), p. 103.

20.   Ibid., p. 117.

21.   Lefebvre, *The Production of Space,* p. 138.

22.   The umbilical connection between designer and dweller is apparent in the concept of a living body; that it is a *radical proposition* may be less apparent: to the dweller because it is too evident (that there is a connection), and to the architect because he or she is blinded by form.

23. The aim is not to dismiss the importance or genius of master architects. Kahn and Gehry are of great significance to our culture, and there will be others. But our obsession with the stars prohibits the appreciation of all others: an underestimated force of architectural culture, whose contribution may have its day in the metropolis. Among well-known architects, Philip Johnson and Rem Koolhaas (despite their sizable egos and heroic postures) take a position closer to the more anonymous architects who are my concern here. Johnson's work, despite all the fanfare, rarely takes the front line, serving rather as a backdrop by its explicit rhetoric and open acknowledgment of its formal roots. Koolhaas's work is a brilliant elaboration on the 50s, and by displaying its heritage—its makeup—steps back, to foreground metropolitan life.

24. Charles Siebert, "My Father's Machines," *New York Times Magazine*, September 27, 1997, p. 91.

25. J. G. Ballard, *A User's Guide to the Millennium: Essays and Reviews* (London: Picador, 1996), p. 276.

26. Ibid.

27. Ibid., p. 279.

28. Jennifer Golub, *Albert Frey/Houses 1+2* (New York: Princeton Architectural Press, 1998), p. 47.

29. In 1949 Borges published a collection of *ficciones* called *El Aleph*. For me most of Borges's fictions are so realistic as to question their label. In the Aleph he wrote: "Carlos Argentino . . . launched into an *apologia* for modern man. 'I picture him,' he said, 'in his study, as though in the watchtower of a great city [28th floor?], surrounded by telephones, telegraphs, phonographs, the latest in radio-telephone and motion-picture and magic-lantern equipment [add Internet, computers, etc.], and glossaries and calendars and time tables and bulletins . . .' this twentieth century of ours had upended the fable of Muhammad and the mountain—mountains nowadays did in fact come to the modern Muhammad." And finally the aleph itself: "Yes, the place where, without admixture or confusion, all the places of the world, seen from every angle, coexist." In *Jorge Luis Borges: Collected Fictions,* trans. Andrew Hurley (New York: Viking Penguin, 1988), pp. 275–276, 281.

30. Foucault suggests that we may eventually refer to the twentieth century as the Deleuzean century in *Language, Counter-memory, Practice: Selected Essays and Interviews by Michel Foucault,* ed. Donald F. Bouchard (Ithaca: Cornell University Press, 1977), p. 165.

31. Gilles Deleuze, *The Logic of Sense,* ed. Constantin V. Boundas, trans. Mark Lester with Charles Stivale (New York: Columbia University Press, 1990), p. 280.

32. Ibid., p. 263.

33. It is worth noting that predictions about the future of politics suggest that direct democracy is in the making because of the Internet. Dick Morris, the political consultant, predicts

that voters using the Internet will make their opinions heard to such a degree that Congress and its special interests will lose their current significance. The voting pool, the chat group, and the design dungeon will be the new marketplace.

34. Castells defines network enterprise as one in which "the actual unit of production is not a firm. It is an ad hoc combination of firms of different sizes and different sectors with different purposes" (p. 8).

35. Robert Goodman, *After the Planners* (New York: Simon and Schuster, 1971), p. 210.

36. Herbert Muschamp, *Man about Town: Frank Lloyd Wright in New York City* (Cambridge: MIT Press, 1983), p. 187. Note Muschamp's remarks about Wright's "everywhere/nowhere ambiguities."

37. Paul and Percival Goodman, *Communitas: Means of Livelihood and Ways of Life* (New York: Morningside Bookshop, 1990).

38. Ilya Prigogine, "The Rediscovery of Value and the Opening of Economics," in *Center* 10, ed. Michael Benedikt (Austin: Center for the Study of American Architecture, University of Texas at Austin, 1997), pp. 1–7.

39. Ibid., p. 4.

40. Ibid., p. 7.

41. Mihaly Csikszentmihalyi, "Values and Socio-Cultural Evolution," in *Center* 10, ed. Benedikt, p. 42.

42. Ibid., pp. 41–42.

43. Ibid., pp. 43–46.

44. Csikszentmihalyi takes the example of the value of being thin rather than fat in modern Western societies, implying that there are other societies where being fat is a sign of wealth and beauty.

45. Michael O'Hare, "Attention, Value, and Exchange," in *Center* 10, ed. Benedikt, p. 85.

46. Csikszentmihalyi, "Values and Socio-Cultural Evolution," p. 50.

47. A work critical of the disciplinary divisions that had prevailed since Aristotle's treatises with the same name: *Organon* (here in Greek).

48. Samuel Beckett, *Watt* (New York: Grove Press, 1959), p. 68.

49. Ibid., pp. 204–205.

50. Jean Baudrillard, *Simulations,* trans. Paul Foss, Paul Patton, and Philip Beitchman (New York: Semiotext(e), 1983), p. 92.

51.   Beckett, *Watt,* p. 187.

52.   Ibid., pp. 160–161.

53.   François Jullien, *The Propensity of Things: Toward a History of Efficacy in China,* trans. Janet Lloyd (New York: Zone Books, 1995).

54.   Ralph Waldo Emerson, *The Complete Works of Ralph Waldo Emerson*, 12 vols., ed. Edward Waldo Emerson (Boston: Houghton, 1903–1904), "Nature," from the First and Second Series, p. 389.

IV The New Frontier

1.   Reyner Banham, *Los Angeles: The Architecture of Four Ecologies* (New York: Penguin Books, 1973).

2.   Walter Benjamin, *Reflections: Essays, Aphorisms, Autobiographical Writings,* ed. Peter Demetz, trans. Edmund Jephcott (New York: Harcourt Brace Jovanovich, 1978), p. 26.

3.   Michel de Certeau, *The Practice of Everyday Life,* trans. Steven F. Rendall (Berkeley: University of California Press, 1984), p. 201.

4.   Ibid., p. 120.

5.   The subjectivity roaming the middle landscape is in favor of an open city, against hard enclaves, for a complete grid, for double reading, ambiguity, interpretation, trespassing, permeability, indeterminancy—the holey plane, *le terrain vague*, the Laconian field.

6.   The Menil Collection should not be confused with the University of St. Thomas, where Philip Johnson designed a copy of University of Virginia à la Mies; what is perplexing is that the Menil is much more Jeffersonian in spirit if not in form.

7.   The museum store has been carefully placed outside the museum in the bordering block, to demonstrate that the museum comes first and the mercantile far behind.

8.   The color was chosen by Mrs. de Menil and her Houston architect Howard Barnstone, whose creative genius often took form in modern, scaled projects.

9.   As might be expected from the Texas Medical Center, the design of the Medical Museum is probably even worse than that of a typical suburban hotel. Doctors, the clients of the new museum, are becoming so increasingly specialized and narrow in outlook that all larger cultural aspirations have been left behind. Knowing everything there is to know about the left ventricle seems to foreclose an interest in the entire architecture of the body or—even further removed—of the buildings the ventricle is supposed to operate in.

10.   This idea is drawn from Gianni Vattimo's *End of Modernity*, in which he suggests that one of the few ways out of the many complex dilemmas of modernity is to fictionalize one's experience. In this book I have applied the idea as a planning concept, thus suggesting that the Museum District should help build a "life of art" for the visitors.

11.   See Adrian Beukers and Ed van Hinte's *Lightness: The Inevitable Renaissance of Minimum Energy Structures* (Rotterdam: 010 Publishers, 1998), p. 30, in particular "How to build a tree": "It is only recently that we have realized that a tree does know a thing or two. Among other subtleties, the wood in various parts of the trunk grows in such a way that it is prestressed. The mechanism behind this is not entirely clear."

12.   Erich Auerbach, *Mimesis: The Representation of Reality in Western Literature,* trans. Willard R. Trask (Princeton: Princeton University Press, 1953), whose excursions inspire work on the mimetic, writes: "then the sensory occurrence pales before the power of the figural meaning" (p. 42).

13.   Frederick Turner, "Biology and Beauty," in Jonathan Crary and Sanford Kwinter, eds., *Incorporations* (New York: Zone, 1992), p. 407.

14.   Gilles Deleuze, *Bergsonism,* trans. Hugh Tomlinson and Barbara Habberjam (New York: Zone Books, 1988), p. 95.

15.   Turner, "Biology and Beauty," p. 406 (quoting Thomas Mann's *The Magic Mountain*).

16.   Claude Lévi-Strauss, *Tristes Tropiques* (New York: Atheneum, 1974), p. 124.

17.   Richard Korn, "The Private Citizen, the Social Expert, and the Social Problem: An Excursion through an Unacknowledged Utopia," in Bernard Rosenberg, Israel Gerver, and F. William Howton, eds., *Mass Society in Crisis* (New York: Macmillan, 1964), p. 579.

18.   "Transportation is in a very cool spot between a social system and a physical system," explains Christopher L. Barrett at Los Alamos National Laboratory. His colleague Steen Rasmussen adds, "The elements [or vehicles widely distributed over space] that interact with one another are like biological systems. They are dynamical hierarchies with controls at many different levels, like organelles, cells, tissues, humans." (Drawn from Kenneth R. Howard, "Unjamming Traffic with Computers," *Scientific American*, October 1997, p. 87.)

Bibliography

Arendt, Hannah. *The Human Condition.* Chicago: University of Chicago Press, 1958.

Auerbach, Erich. *Mimesis: The Representation of Reality in Western Literature.* Trans. Willard R. Trask. Princeton: Princeton University Press, 1953.

Ballard, J. G. *A User's Guide to the Millennium: Essays and Reviews.* London: Picador, 1996.

Banham, Reyner. *Los Angeles: The Architecture of Four Ecologies.* New York: Penguin Books, 1973.

Barthes, Roland. *The Pleasure of the Text.* Trans. Richard Miller. New York: Hill & Wang, 1975.

Baudrillard, Jean. *America.* Trans. Chris Turner. New York: Verso, 1988.

Baudrillard, Jean. *Simulations.* Trans. Paul Foss, Paul Patton, and Philip Beitchman. New York: Semiotext(e), 1983.

Beckett, Samuel. *Watt.* New York: Grove Press, 1959.

Bell, David. "Knowledge and the Middle Landscape: Jefferson's University of Virginia." *Journal of Architectural Education,* 37, no. 2 (Winter 1983), 18–26.

Benedikt, Michael, senior ed. *Center* 10. Austin: Center for the Study of American Architecture, University of Texas at Austin, 1997.

Benjamin, Walter. *Illuminations: Essays and Reflections.* Ed. Hannah Arendt. Trans. Harry Zohn. New York: Schocken Books, 1969.

Benjamin, Walter. *Reflections: Essays, Aphorisms, Autobiographical Writings.* Ed. Peter Demetz. Trans. Edmund Jephcott. New York: Harcourt Brace Jovanovich, 1978.

Beukers, Adrian, and Ed van Hinte. *Lightness: The Inevitable Renaissance of Minimum Energy Structures.* Rotterdam: 010 Publishers, 1998.

Borges, Jorge Luis. *Labyrinths: Selected Stories and Other Writings.* Ed. Donald A. Yates and James E. Irby. New York: New Directions, 1964.

Borges, Jorge Luis. *Jorge Luis Borges: Collected Fictions.* Trans. Andrew Hurley. New York: Viking Penguin, 1988.

Bouchard, D. F., ed. *Language, Counter-memory, Practice: Selected Essays and Interviews by Michel Foucault.* Ithaca: Cornell University Press, 1977.

Bryson, Norman. "The Gaze in the Expanded Field." In Hal Foster, ed., *Vision and Visuality.* Seattle: Bay Press, 1988.

Cacciari, Massimo. *Architecture and Nihilism: On the Philosophy of Modern Architecture.*

Trans. Stephen Sartarelli. New Haven: Yale University Press, 1993.

Clay, Grady. *Real Places: An Unconventional Guide to America's Generic Landscape.* Chicago: University of Chicago Press, 1994.

Certeau, Michel de. *The Practice of Everyday Life.* Trans. Steven F. Rendall. Berkeley: University of California Press, 1984.

Deleuze, Gilles. *Bergsonism.* Trans. Hugh Tomlinson and Barbara Habberjam. New York: Zone Books, 1988.

Deleuze, Gilles. *The Fold: Leibniz and the Baroque.* Trans. Tom Conley. Minneapolis: University of Minnesota Press, 1993.

Deleuze, Gilles. *Foucault.* Ed. and trans. Seán Hand. Minneapolis: University of Minnesota Press, 1988.

Deleuze, Gilles. *The Logic of Sense.* Ed. Constantin V. Boundas. Trans. Mark Lester with Charles Stivale. New York: Columbia University Press, 1990.

Deleuze, Gilles, and Félix Guattari. *A Thousand Plateaus: Capitalism and Schizophrenia.* Trans. Brian Massumi. Minneapolis: University of Minnesota Press, 1987.

Deleuze, Gilles, and Claire Parnet. *Dialogues.* Trans. Hugh Tomlinson and Barbara Habberjam. New York: Columbia University Press, 1987.

Derrida, Jacques. *Of Grammatology.* Trans. Gayatri Chakravorty Spivak. Baltimore: Johns Hopkins University Press, 1976.

Downs, Anthony. *New Visions for Metropolitan America.* Washington: Brookings Institution; Cambridge: Lincoln Institute of Land Policy, 1994.

Eco, Umberto. *A Theory of Semiotics.* Bloomington: Indiana University Press, 1979.

Emerson, Ralph Waldo. *The Complete Works of Ralph Waldo Emerson.* 12 vols. Ed. Edward Waldo Emerson. Boston: Houghton, 1903–1904. "Nature," from the First and Second series.

Ferry, Luc. *The New Ecological Order.* Trans. Carol Volk. Chicago: University of Chicago Press, 1995.

Focillon, Henri. *The Life of Forms in Art.* Trans. Charles Beecher Hogan and George Kubler. New York: Zone Books, 1989.

Foucault, Michel. *Discipline and Punish: The Birth of the Prison.* Trans. Alan Sheridan. New York: Random House, 1979.

Foucault, Michel. *The Order of Things: An Archaeology of the Human Sciences.* New York: Random House, 1970.

Gibson, William. *Mona Lisa Overdrive.* New York: Bantam Books, 1988.

Glassie, Henry. *Folk Housing in Middle Virginia.* Knoxville: University of Tennessee Press, 1975.

Golub, Jennifer. *Albert Frey/Houses 1+2.* New York: Princeton Architectural Press, 1998.

Goodman, Paul and Percival. *Communitas: Means of Livelihood and Ways of Life.* New York: Morningside Bookshop, 1990.

Goodman, Robert. *After the Planners.* New York: Simon and Schuster, 1971.

Guattari, Félix. *Chaosophy.* Ed. S. Lotringer. New York: Semiotext(e), 1995.

Hall, E. T. *The Hidden Dimension.* New York: Anchor Books: 1990.

Hollier, Denis. *Against Architecture: The Writings of Georges Bataille.* Trans. Betsy Wing. Cambridge: MIT Press, 1989.

Holt, Nancy, ed. *The Writings of Robert Smithson.* New York: New York University Press, 1979.

Howard, Kenneth R. "Unjamming Traffic with Computers." *Scientific American*, October 1997.

Jackson, J. B. "The Westward-Moving House." In *Landscapes: Selected Writing of J. B. Jackson,* ed. Erwin H. Zube. Amherst: University of Massachusetts Press, 1970.

Jackson, Kenneth T. *Crabgrass Frontier: The Suburbanization of the United States.* New York: Oxford University Press, 1985.

Judd, Donald. *Architektur.* Münster: Westfälischer Kunstverein, 1989.

Jullien, François. *The Propensity of Things: Toward a History of Efficacy in China.* Trans. Janet Lloyd. New York: Zone Books, 1995.

Korn, Richard. "The Private Citizen, the Social Expert, and the Social Problem: An Excursion through an Unacknowledged Utopia." In Bernard Rosenberg, Israel Gerver, and F. William Howton, eds., *Mass Society in Crisis.* New York: Macmillan, 1964.

Krieger, Martin. *Doing Physics: How Physicists Take Hold of the World.* Bloomington: Indiana University Press, 1992.

Lang, Peter, and Tam Miller, eds. *Suburban Discipline.* New York: Princeton Architectural Press, 1997.

Lefebvre, Henri. *The Production of Space.* Trans. Donald Nicholson-Smith. Oxford: Blackwell, 1991.

Lerup, Lars. "At the End of the Architectural Promenade." In Scott Marble et al., eds., *Architecture and Body.* New York: Rizzoli, 1988.

Lerup, Lars. *Building the Unfinished: Architecture and Human Action.* Beverly Hills: Sage Publications, 1977.

Lerup, Lars. "Hands Up." In Dung Ngo, ed., *Louis I. Kahn: Coversations with Students.* Architecture @ Rice 26. Houston: Rice School of Architecture, 1988.

Lerup, Lars. "Stim & Dross: Rethinking the Metropolis." *Assemblage* (Cambridge: MIT Press, 1994).

Lévi-Strauss, Claude. *Tristes Tropiques* New York: Atheneum: 1974.

Lynch, Kevin. *The Image of the City.* Cambridge, Mass.: Technology Press, 1960.

MacDonald, William L. *The Pantheon: Design, Meaning, and Progeny.* Cambridge: Harvard University Press, 1976.

Maffesoli, Michel. *The Time of the Tribes: The Decline of Individualism in Mass Society.* Trans. Don Smith. London: Sage Publications, 1996.

Merleau-Ponty, Maurice. *Phenomenology of Perception.* Trans. Colin Smith. London: Routledge & Kegan Paul; New York: Humanities Press, 1962.

Miller, Perry. *Errand into the Wilderness.* Cambridge: Harvard University Press, 1956.

Minsky, Marvin. *The Society of Mind.* Cambridge: MIT Press, 1988.

Muschamp, Herbert. *Man about Town: Frank Lloyd Wright in New York City.* Cambridge: MIT Press, 1983.

Rossi, Aldo. *The Architecture of the City.* Cambridge: MIT Press, 1982.

Serres, Michel. *Rome: The Book of Foundations.* Trans. Felicia McCarren. Stanford: Stanford University Press, 1991.

Storper, Michael. "Beautiful Cities, Ugly Cities: Urban Form as Convention." In Michael Benedikt, ed., *Center* 10. Austin: Center for the Study of American Architecture, University of Texas at Austin, 1997.

Suzuki, Daisetz T. *Zen and Japanese Culture.* Princeton: Princeton University Press, 1959.

Tafuri, Manfredo. *Architecture and Utopia: Design and Capitalist Development.* Trans. Barbara Luigia La Penta. Cambridge: MIT Press, 1976.

Thucydides. *History of the Peloponnesian War.* Trans. Rex Warner. Baltimore: Penguin Books, 1954.

Turner, Frederick. "Biology and Beauty." In Jonathan Crary and Sanford Kwinter, eds., *Incorporations*. New York: Zone, 1992.

Tzonis, Alexander, and Liane Lefaivre. *Classical Architecture: The Poetics of Order*. Cambridge: MIT Press, 1986.

Vaneigem, Raoul. *The Movement of the Free Spirit*. Trans. Randall Cherry and Ian Patterson. New York: Zone Books, 1994.

Vattimo, Gianni. *The End of Modernity: Nihilism and Hermeneutics in Postmodern Culture*. Trans. Jon R. Snyder. Baltimore: Johns Hopkins University Press, 1991.

Virilio, Paul. *The Vision Machine*. Trans. Julie Rose. Bloomington: Indiana University Press, 1994.

Vlach, John Michael. *Back of the Big House: The Architecture of Plantation Slavery*. Chapel Hill: University of North Carolina Press, 1993.

Wycherley, R. E. *How the Greeks Built Cities*. New York: W. W. Norton, 1962.

Illustration Credits

Figures 1, 3
Photographs by Paul Hester, © Paul Hester

Figure 2
Photograph courtesy of the DLR Group

Figures 4, 7
Photographs by Steve Brady

Figure 5
Photograph by Esther Bubley

Figures 6, 8, 10, 14
Photographs by George O. Jackson

Figure 9
Photograph by Geoff Winningham

Figures 11, 26
Photographs by Luke Bulman and Kimberly Shoemake

Figures 12, 13
Drawn by Lars Lerup, 1994

Figure 15
Collage by Bruce Webb; photograph by Paul Hester

Figure 16
Courtesy of the Texas Department of Transportation

Figure 17
Unknown

Figure 18
From Waldemar Titzenthaler, *Berlin in Photographien des 19. Jahrhunderts,* ed. Friedrich Terveen (Berlin: Rembrandt Verlag, 1968), p. 69

Figure 19
From Karl Friedrich Schinkel, *Collection of Architectural Designs* (New York: Princeton Architectural Press, 1989)

Figures 20, 21
© Fondation Le Corbusier

Figure 22
Drawn by Lars Lerup, 1986

Figure 23
From Le Corbusier, *Urbanisme,* 1930, © Fondation Le Corbusier—L3(1)5

Figure 25
Photograph from the exhibition "The Eichler Homes: Building the California Dream," University of Texas, Austin, 1998

Figure 27
Drawn by Patrick Winters

Figure 28
From Lars Lerup, *Planned Assaults* (Montreal: Centre Canadien d'Architecture/Canadian Centre for Architecture, 1987), drawn by Hassan Afrookhteh

Figure 29
Lars Lerup, 1986

Figure 30
Drawn by Luke Bulman

Figure 31
Photograph by Angela Loughry and Kevin Guarnotta

Figures 32–40
Photographs by Ben Thorne

Figure 41
Drawn by Luke Bulman and Kimberly Shoemake

Figure 42
Photograph by Onezieme Mouton

Figure 43
Drawn by Lars Lerup

Index